Teach® Yourself

Get Your Child into the School You Want

Katie Krais

For UK order enquiries: please contact Bookpoint Ltd,
130 Milton Park, Abingdon, Oxon OX14 4SB.
Telephone: +44 (0) 1235 827720. Fax: +44 (0) 1235 400454.
Lines are open 09.00–17.00, Monday to Saturday, with a 24-hour
message answering service. Details about our titles and how to
order are available at www.teachyourself.com

Long renowned as the authoritative source for self-guided learning –
with more than 50 million copies sold worldwide – the **Teach Yourself**
series includes over 500 titles in the fields of languages, crafts, hobbies,
business, computing and education.

British Library Cataloguing in Publication Data: a catalogue record
for this title is available from the British Library.

First published in UK 2009 by Hodder Education, part of
Hachette UK, 338 Euston Road, London NW1 3BH.

This edition published 2010.

Previously published as *Teach Yourself Getting Your Child into
Secondary School.*

The **Teach Yourself** name is a registered trade mark of
Hodder Headline.

Typeset by MPS Limited, a Macmillan Company.

Printed in Great Britain for Hodder Education, an Hachette UK
Company, 338 Euston Road, London NW1 3BH, by CPI Cox &
Wyman, Reading, Berkshire RG1 8EX.

The publisher has used its best endeavours to ensure that the URLs
for external websites referred to in this book are correct and active
at the time of going to press. However, the publisher and the
author have no responsibility for the websites and can make no
guarantee that a site will remain live or that the content will remain
relevant, decent or appropriate.

Hachette UK's policy is to use papers that are natural, renewable
and recyclable products and made from wood grown in sustainable
forests. The logging and manufacturing processes are expected to
conform to the environmental regulations of the country of origin.

Impression number   10 9 8 7 6 5 4 3 2 1
Year   2014 2013 2012 2011 2010

Acknowledgements

A big thank you to my gorgeous children Daisy and Holly as well as my wonderful husband and 'editor' Howard, for your love, encouragement and patience.

Get Your Child into the School You Want

Contents

Meet the author

Having worked in industry for four years, after graduating with a degree in psychology from Southampton University, I decided to enter the rewarding and ever-changing environment known as education.

Nothing quite prepares you for the reality of teaching – the responsibility for the learning of 30 little people. From day one I loved it – the buzz and challenge and the idea that you are actually making a difference. My philosophy was always that children learn better when they are happy and in lessons that are fun and interactive – and if that meant dressing up as an Egyptian princess and performing a mummification then so be it! Some of those children will now be in their early twenties but I am sure they will still remember that lesson.

My career began as a class teacher with experience teaching Years 3, 4, 5 and 6. Since then I have worked as a year group leader, an assessment co-ordinator and a teacher governor. My last four years have been spent as a special needs co-ordinator and member of senior management, providing and managing the appropriate resources to children with special needs.

I have been very involved in working with secondary schools to help with the transition programme from key stage 2 to key stage 3 as well as working closely with infant schools to enable Year 2 children to transfer smoothly to their junior school.

During this time, I also became the mother of Daisy, now 13 and Holly, 10. I always thought that being a teacher would prepare me for the challenges of motherhood – how wrong I was!

The biggest challenge came when my elder daughter was approaching Year 6 and decisions needed to be made about secondary schools. I was very confident that I knew which schools would suit her and what direction to take. However, when we listened to others we found a lot of conflicting advice and many people scaring us with horror stories and gossip which turned out to be ill informed. Feedback from parents' evening suggested our child should sit the entrance exams at the best state selective schools. While I had no doubt my daughter had ability, I just didn't think she was in the top 5% of the country which is where she needed to be to get into these schools. I felt confused during this time – with no one actually telling me the information I wanted and needed to know.

Going through the transition process I realized that parents are not given access to the information they really need to make informed decisions about secondary schools – the main detail being how bright your child is. Teachers are very good at telling you about your child's behaviour, their willingness to partake in a lesson, how well they work in groups with others, but they don't actually tell you where they are academically compared to others in the class and, most importantly, against the national average. This is important information as it provides you with the knowledge you need to make an informed decision about future schooling.

With this experience fresh, I set up my own consultancy called 'Surviving School Transfer', a secondary school transfer consultancy advising parents on all aspects of secondary transfer. Prompted by the success of this consultancy, I went on to write this book.

This book provides first-hand advice to parents on how to survive this stressful secondary transition process, arming them with up-to-date knowledge, facts and rules about the transfer system as well as providing them with realistic expectations about potential schools based on thorough assessments.

In my many roles at school and through my consultancy experience I understand what information parents need to have in order to make an informed judgement about the ability of their children and how to move them forward in order to get the best education available.

In 2010 I set up a new consultancy called 'Jaderberg Krais Educational Consultancy', with my partner Lorrae Jaderberg, offering advice and guidance across all aspects of education.

Only got a minute?

There are three main choices of secondary school for you to consider: state, state selective and private. Entry criteria for these schools vary greatly and it is vital that you can navigate your way through this minefield.

Entry into state schools is co-ordinated by the local authority where you reside. You will be given a Common Application Form (CAF) in September, usually to be completed by mid October, when your child is in Year 6. This asks you to list preferred schools. All schools on your preferred list will be contacted and they will consider giving your child a place based on their respective admissions criteria. They do not know where you have ranked them. If you meet the criteria then your authority will be notified that the school will offer you a place. Once all the schools have responded your local authority will offer you a place at the highest ranking school that has offered you a place. This will happen in the first week of March. If none of your preferred schools offer you a place, then it is the responsibility of your local authority to offer you a place at another school within the authority. They are not obligated to provide you with any of your preferred schools.

Entry into state selective schools is linked to state school entry, but the main admissions criteria are aptitude and ability. Therefore entrance to these schools is usually based on academic performance in an examination.

Private schools operate a completely different system. You will need to apply directly to the individual schools rather than through your local authority. Most private schools will ask your child to sit an exam and this usually takes place between November and February of Year 6. There is also a charge for sitting the exam. Many private schools will also ask your child to undergo an interview. Usually you will find out the results of the private school exams at the end of February when the schools make their offers.

5 Only got five minutes?

The transition from primary to secondary school is a very stressful time – not just for the child but for the parents too. In order to get your child into the school of your choice, you need to make sure that your choices are realistic ones and that you have started to plan the path to secondary school ahead of time.

Know your options and visit the schools

Secondary transition may seem a long way off when your child is seven, but blink and it'll be upon you. It is important to be ahead of the game and understand what's available and what will work for your child and your family. Decisions over state, state selective or private schools can be considered early on.

Know the different types of schools that are out there. Many schools have specialisms, some are religious, some are local community schools. What schools are in your local area? Would you consider sending your child to a private school?

Once you have decided on the type of school that suits your child you need to start shortlisting these schools.

Using the internet, look at schools' websites and brochures, Ofsted results and league table positions. Also look at school profiles, their university places and contact a school Choice Adviser from your local authority to guide you through your choices.

Then you need to visit the schools. First impressions will be very important and you should always listen to your instincts: no one knows your child better than you do. You will also need to be observant during the school tour. Does the school site look cared for, does the head teacher know the children's names and do the children look smart and well behaved? Questions asked during your visit can be very enlightening about the ethos and culture of a school.

Study admissions criteria

Once you have decided on which schools you consider appropriate for your child's secondary education you must then consider a very important question – will your child get in? If a school is not oversubscribed, then the answer will probably be yes. However, many good schools are oversubscribed and there is no point choosing a school if you have no chance of success. The key to success is meeting a school's admissions criteria. If you meet them, you will be offered a place. If you don't meet them, you will not be offered a place, no matter how high up you have placed this school on your preference list.

To find out the admissions criteria for any school you can speak to the relevant local authority admissions team or you can look at the school's website. Admissions criteria may be based on a number of factors, such as aptitude, religion, sibling attendance or geography, and it's important to check what these are.

Know your deadlines and procedures

Deadlines for application forms to secondary school do vary across the country and indeed from year to year. Up-to-date information is always found on your local authority website or by contacting schools direct. For the majority of schools the Common Application Form (CAF) needs to be completed by the middle of October when your child is in Year 6. For some schools, you might need to fill in additional forms and give additional supporting material. Deadlines are strict – if you do not submit your application in time it will affect your chances of a successful place.

10 Only got ten minutes?

The fact that you are reading this book is a good indication that you are aware how hard it is to get your child into a good school. Whether your child is still at infant school or if secondary transition is looming there is certain information you need to know in order to make an informed judgement.

Choosing which school

It is very important to find out what types of schools are available and which schools will suit your child. Some children prefer larger schools, some smaller. There can be advantages and disadvantages of going to a single-sex school or a co-educational school. Some schools will offer GCSEs and A levels, while others will offer the International Baccalaureate (IB).

Once you have decided on the right school for your child, you then need to see how your child can gain entrance in Year 7. State schools are non-fee paying schools with class sizes of around 30 children. The admissions process is run by your local authority and if a school is oversubscribed then they will provide places based on priority for meeting their admissions criteria.

It is crucial to know if your child meets the admissions criteria. You will be asked by your local authority to give school preferences on their CAF. If you choose a school where your child does not meet the criteria then it is a wasted choice. You would be surprised how many boys apply for a girls' school because their parents don't realize that it is a single-sex school – they have only looked at the league tables and want their son to go to a high ranking school!

Finding out the ability level of your child

For private and state selective schools, much of your child's success will depend on their ability to pass an academic test. For the private sector, this will include an interview as well.

You will need to know two things: firstly how clever your child is and secondly how clever they need to be to get into certain schools.

Never assume that because your child is in the top group in the class for maths and English, that they will automatically be good enough to get into your chosen school. They may be top of their class, but how does their class compare to others? To find this out ask your child's teacher for the National Curriculum teacher assessment level for your child in maths, English writing and English reading. You can use this score to identify how your child compares with the national average. Also useful are standardized scores for verbal and non-verbal reasoning tests. These assess a child's potential and for many schools are the first types of test they administer at the 11+.

Subjects tested at the 11+

Maths and English are tested by most schools at the 11+ level. Most aspects of these subjects are covered within key stage 2 of the National Curriculum, so very little should come as a surprise. In most primary schools children will have experience of writing stories, answering comprehension type questions and working on maths papers. However, the big difference comes with the verbal and non-verbal reasoning tests which are not taught within the National Curriculum. These tests often need to be prepared for outside of school. This may happen through a tutor or with parental support using practice materials available at leading bookstores.

Many private schools will want to interview your child and possibly you as well. State selective schools are not allowed to do this. Sometimes these interviews are one to one, sometimes they are in pairs and sometimes they are in a group. They may focus on straightforward questions, or on problem solving or group tasks. It is often useful to spend time with your child going through possible questions so they can think about what their responses might be.

How to prepare your child for the tests

Supporting your child through the whole 11+ process can be a difficult one to judge. On the one hand you want to give them the best possible practice and for them to be as prepared as they can be. Thus tutoring your child from an early age may seem a very sensible idea. However, you need to make sure you are tutoring for the right reasons. If a child needs a great deal of one-to-one tutoring in order for them to pass the exams, then you might question why you are putting them forward for the exams in the first place. Hot housing your child may in the short term gain them access to this treasured school, but once they are there they will soon become disillusioned and frustrated as they struggle to keep up with the pace set by others. Therefore tutoring should be simply a way of ironing out the academic creases rather than brainwashing a child with difficult ideas and concepts. It should also be teaching children about examination technique.

What to do if it all goes wrong

If you have not been successful in securing the school you want for your child it is always possible to appeal. This takes place through your local authority. A word of caution – very few appeals are successful. As long as a school can prove they have followed the guidelines of their admissions policy and that your child did not meet their criteria once they were oversubscribed then there are very few circumstances which would enable the school's ruling to be overturned.

Therefore it is extremely important to plan well ahead of time and make sure the schools that you put down are attainable and reasonable. You might find that the only way to ensure a place at the school of your choice is to sell your house and buy a new one plumb in the middle of the school's catchment area. You won't be the first to do this, and you won't be the last!

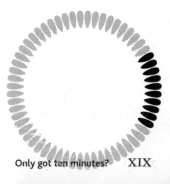

1

Getting started

In this chapter you will learn:

- *why secondary transfer is a difficult and confusing time for many parents*
- *why parents often feel uninformed about their child's academic abilities*
- *how to use this book to help you through every stage of school transfer.*

> ## Expert opinion: the admissions process
>
> 'The complex process for school admissions is made impenetrable by the tangle of myths that weave themselves around it. As a head teacher, I often find myself working hard to understand every nuance of the process: I can only sympathize with the thousands of parents who try to untangle it every year.'
>
> Martin Post, Headmaster of Watford Grammar School for Boys, a partially selective state secondary school in Hertfordshire

Getting a child into secondary school is the single biggest educational challenge facing most parents of children aged 7–11. It is an incredibly thorny issue, and one that is frequently discussed in playgrounds and dinner parties, often leading to 'Chinese whispers' where information is embellished, exaggerated or simply incorrect by the time it gets to your ears.

Our school system is incredibly confusing. The choice is potentially wide – state or independent, mixed or single sex, local or in another borough, grammar, crammer, faith, boarding, special needs... Parents are required to visit many of these, fill in a multitude of confusing forms, navigate the 'catchment areas *vs* house prices' dilemma, supervise practice papers with their child, and stay sane. Parents often feel 'overwhelmed' by the process – from knowing what is available, to finding the most appropriate school for their particular child, to supporting their child through the process. During this anxious time when children need encouragement, help and extra confidence, they also need calm parents who have done their homework too.

Parent case study

'I found the whole process of transferring my daughter to secondary school overwhelming. Other parents told me that if my child was to stand any chance of getting into the local selective state school she should have been seeing a tutor since at least Year 4. Her class teacher has told me she is bright, but is she bright enough?'

Holly, mother of Kate (Year 6)

When does the secondary school worry begin?

From the very first educational stepping stones, parents often fret about their child's abilities and future. Confusion first emerges around the time of playgroups and nursery when emotions take control and the desire to have your child be the first (or at least not the last) to reach each significant developmental milestone sets in. How soon it seems that Reception, the introductory year at school, is upon you. Does your child play appropriately in the sand pit? Did they change into their PE kit independently without bursting into tears? Was it unrealistic to try to teach them to tie their shoelaces? Then onto Year 1, when the education of our darlings begins for real – this is the big time; at the tender age of five things get serious. Your child can continue their gymnastics, ballet, swimming, violin, football, cooking and drama clubs but now they need to concentrate on writing, reading and counting as well. Pressure, pressure, pressure!

Expert opinion: secondary school transfer

'I am always surprised how early worry over secondary schools comes – worry over secondary transfer can start even before a child starts infant school. It is very common for parents to ask me about local secondary schools when they visit my school for the first time prior to application for Reception or Nursery places. They even start to ask about the best time to start tutoring.

Although I advise against tutoring as I feel it is inappropriate for such young children, some parents employ private tutors for their children as early as Year 1 or send them to "reading clubs" or Kumon. Parents do this for a variety of reasons; one of these is concern about future secondary transfer and the availability of places. This concern leads some parents to apply to the private sector at the transition to key stage 2, in order to secure a place early and avoid the "11+ rush". The number who do so varies from year to year. However since summer 2008, parents are obliged to apply for entry to the junior school for their children, as transfer is not now automatic. This causes concern for many parents who, on applying to the infant school, expected a smooth transition to the junior school. This is, in itself, unsettling and may well affect parents' future decisions about transfer to key stage 2 and this will impact on their secondary school choices.'

Head teacher of a state community school in London

No one tells you what you need to know

By Year 3 your child is in junior school, following the key stage 2 curriculum. It is no longer enough just to know if your child is happy and sociable. You also want to know if they are academic. Unfortunately, this information is not always easily available. At parents' evenings it is easy to hear that your child is delightful. It comes as no surprise that they are kind. The knowledge that they are chatty in class, easily distracted and daydream occasionally may also not be a shock. You already know this! What becomes frustrating is that teachers won't answer the important questions, such as: Is your child clever? If so, how clever?

Insight

I found that at every parents' evening I was told my daughter was doing really well and was in the top groups for maths and English. With hindsight, this was not enough for her to get into a state selective school. Top group isn't enough – it has to be top of the top group.

You may also want to know how your child is performing compared with the rest of the class. Of course the teachers would never divulge such information, and nor should they. Nonetheless, it can be frustrating not knowing exactly how your child is doing against the pack of wolves she calls her friends! If you are considering sitting your child for entrance exams you need to know if this is a worthwhile exercise or completely unrealistic. No matter how relaxed you are, no matter how keen you are to allow your child to develop at her own pace, you can't help but be influenced by the growing climate of competitiveness at school.

As termly or annual parents' evenings become increasingly woolly, additional information is given to parents in the shape of end of year reports. These are often full of information about what your child *can* do: '... she can round two-digit or three-digit numbers to the nearest 10 or 100'; '... he can order dates in chronological order'; '... she can explain why it is important to look after her teeth'. They will also be saturated with comments about what your child *enjoyed*: '… she enjoyed learning about the Tudors'; '… he enjoyed his trip to the Hindu Mandir'. Nonetheless, these reports still do not give the concrete information you need in order to make an informed decision about the correct secondary school for your child.

As my daughter neared Year 7 it was clear I needed to start asking questions about life beyond the comfortable existence of junior school. Where should I start? Was it already too late? Where would be the best place to send her? I knew a little about the supposed reputations of some of the schools nearby – at least, I knew what my friends and acquaintances told me – but I quickly became aware that I knew very little about this big event fast approaching us. I had no idea what to do, where to start, where to go for advice; most importantly I really didn't know what school would best suit my child's abilities and personality. This is important, and a decision you have to get right as it will shape your child's future.

I searched – but failed – to find some materials to help me, so I set about researching the 'whats, wheres and hows' of secondary school transfer; first of all for my own child and our particular situation, then to help other friends and parents at school. I realized that the bank of information I was acquiring could be put to good use, so I set up a secondary school consultancy to give structured advice to parents. And so it led to this book: a book I would have given my right arm for when my first child was approaching the end of primary school.

Did you know?

▶ *Over half a million children transfer to secondary schools each year, of which 40,000 go into the independent sector.*
▶ *15% of parents do not gain their first-choice school; in London this figure rises to 28%.*

(Contd)

> ▶ *20% of parents are not satisfied with the choice of schools in their area. This figure is higher in London even though there are more schools to choose from.*
>
> Figures from research commissioned by the Department for Children,
> Schools and Families (February 2008)

How this book can help

We all want our children to thrive and be happy in the right school environment. We also want our children to get into the schools we feel are right for them. The aim of this book is to ease the panic, to deal with the scaremongering, to keep parents calm and grounded in a mad school system and to provide you with tools and information. You are not alone; there are thousands of parents who feel just as confused and anxious as you do. Emotions – particularly those concerning your children – are very powerful and can potentially cloud good judgement. This book will allow you to rise above the trauma and perhaps even enjoy this next stage in your child's school career.

It turns out there is no mystique to secondary transfer success when you know how to play the game. The fact is there are not many people around who can offer the support or guidance that parents require during these painful months. Whether transferring to comprehensive, selective or private schools there are set procedures to follow, hoops to jump, forms to fill in and deadlines to meet. While these can change slightly from year to year, the process fundamentally remains the same… except it seems that every year it gets ever more competitive.

This book is packed with clever hints and tips to steer you through the whole process with relative ease. It includes:

▶ *advice on how to prepare your child academically for success in secondary school tests and interviews*

- ▶ *tips for helping you and your child cope with exam-day nerves*
- ▶ *an overview of all the different types of schools available and how to apply*
- ▶ *a checklist of things to do and think about in each school year so that you are ahead of the game*
- ▶ *a guide to assessing the academic ability of your child compared to the national average*
- ▶ *how to work out which school will suit your child on both an academic and a pastoral level*
- ▶ *how to draw up a shortlist – where to research schools and what information you should count and discount*
- ▶ *how to fill in the local authority and individual school forms – does ranking really count?*
- ▶ *advice for children with special needs and statements*
- ▶ *information and guidance about the dreaded appeal process*
- ▶ *practical tips in helping your child get ready for the changes at secondary school in terms of both organization and confidence.*

In short, it will tell you everything you need to know about the secondary transfer process. So, whether you carry it around for a quick glance when you are sitting on a train or waiting to pick up the kids from school, or whether you study it in those few stolen moments in the bath or in bed, you should use this book as an essential read to dip in and out of whenever you feel the need. Secondary transfer is not something you can deal with quickly in its entirety; you need to revisit this book as each new question arises or you move onto a new stage of the transition journey.

There is nothing better in life than feeling in control. It is my hope that once you have read this book you will feel confident and ready to conquer the educational maelstrom known as secondary transfer.

Good luck, and remember: it *is* rocket science – don't trust anyone who tells you otherwise!

Expert opinion: remain positive

'As the head teacher of a thriving and successful girls' school in north London, and also the mother of four sons, I feel well placed to offer advice on the sometimes very stressful process that is the 11+ transfer. I want to emphasize that in all likelihood your son or daughter will sit down in September of Year 7 at a wonderful school! Secondary schools are all on the same journey, that is, to make sure that all pupils fulfil their potential and take their place as happy, contributing citizens. Your attitude to schools will inevitably colour your child's view, so it is important not to set your heart on one school alone. If you are reading this book, you have shown you are committed to doing the best for your child: he or she is very lucky, as you are their most important educators. Wherever they go, you will need to support them, nurture them, and reassure them that they are in a great environment that is right for them.'

Barbara Elliott, Head teacher of Channing School, a private girls' secondary school in London

2

Understanding the different types of secondary schools

In this chapter you will learn:
- *about the different types of schools available*
- *the importance of admissions criteria and how these differ for each type of school*
- *a checklist of things to do and think about in each school year.*

It was simpler for our parents. Educational choices were clear. If you had money you could go private. If you had brains you could go to a grammar. Otherwise you would go to the local comprehensive – some were excellent, others weren't. Nowadays there are so many different types of secondary schools you need a master's degree just to tell them apart and understand their differences. Don't worry if you get confused – you are not alone. It's hard to tell the difference between a special school and a specialist school, a voluntary aided school and a voluntary controlled school without prior knowledge. While it is important to find out these differences, the most important thing is to find out how these schools differ in their admissions criteria, what forms you need to fill in – and yes, what mountains to climb to ensure your child has the best possible chance of success.

Types of secondary schools

Schools fall into two main categories – private (fee-paying) or state (free).

Private (independent) schools

These are schools that charge fees and control their own admissions, as well as recruit and employ their own staff. There are around 2,600 private schools in England, educating around 671,000 children, which is around 7% of the pupil population. The average termly fee in 2008, according to statistics released by the Independent Schools Council (ISC) was £3023, with school fees typically cheaper in the North and primary preparatory schools.

Local authorities play no role in the application process to these schools – it is completely separate. Parents are advised to find out about these schools themselves. Bursaries are available, as are scholarships. Admissions are based on exams with some exams being easier than others and some schools being easier to get into than others. It is very important to know what level your child is working at so you have realistic expectations with regard to success.

Insight

I found it helpful buying online a selection of private school guide books in order to identify local private schools. Central lists of private schools are not easily available.

For most private schools you apply to each one separately and sit exams at their premises. Some, mainly the girls' schools, have consortiums. This means that one exam can be taken for lots of schools, but you will still need to pay each school for its consideration. An example is the North London Independent Girls' Schools' Consortium where the same exam may be taken for up to nine schools. Most private schools will ask successful candidates back for interview before offering a place. This interview can be conducted on a one-to-one basis, or in a paired or group setting. Some schools change this year on year. Occasionally, parents may be interviewed as well as the child.

Some private schools, for example Harrow School, require children to take an 11+ entrance exam two years before entry to the school at age 13. It is therefore very important to make sure you know when the exams are for each school. Other schools, for example The Haberdashers' Aske's Boys' School, offer entrance exams to the senior school twice, once at 11+ and again at 13+.

State schools

Within the state system, there are lots of subcategories. A list of the most common types of state schools follows.

COMMUNITY SCHOOLS AND COLLEGES

Community schools and colleges are state schools, with all staff employed by the local authority. Similarly, the school's land and buildings are owned by the local authority, which also has primary responsibility for admissions. In other words, these types of school have no discretion when it comes to who they must admit – overall responsibility is with the local authority and the will also arrange appeals for places at these schools.

FOUNDATION SCHOOLS

Staff at foundation schools are employed by the governing body, and it, or a charitable foundation, owns the school's site and premises. The governing body may be made up of parents, representatives of the local authority or representatives of the local community. Foundation schools receive recurrent funding through the local authority, but the primary responsibility for admissions is through the governing body. This means that there may be some kind of 'covert' selection through the admissions criteria and it is important to find out exactly what these criteria are if you want your child to get in.

VOLUNTARY AIDED SCHOOLS

Voluntary aided schools have staff who are employed by the governing body. Land and buildings are normally owned by a charitable foundation, with playing fields generally owned by the local authority. The governing body has primary responsibility for admissions, and usually also contributes a minimum of 10% of any capital project costs. The foundation/trust makes up a majority of the governing body.

These schools are often very appealing to parents because they control their own admissions, and can have specific criteria when it comes to accepting students. Many of these types of schools have a religious connection, and may demand regular attendance at places of worship. Others may not be so strict when it comes to religious commitment.

VOLUNTARY CONTROLLED SCHOOLS

In the case of voluntary controlled schools the local authority employs the school staff and decides on admission procedures. The land and buildings, however, are normally owned by a charitable foundation.

SPECIAL SCHOOLS OR SPECIAL NEEDS SCHOOLS

Special schools are run by the local educational authority for children with special educational needs (SEN). See Chapter 9 for more information. These days there are fewer special schools than in the past, as the government has encouraged an inclusive policy in all mainstream schools, thus creating more opportunity for children with special needs to access the curriculum in a mainstream setting. In addition, some regular schools have additional special needs units attached to them, thus allowing children with more profound special needs to attend a mainstream school but be given specialist teaching, where appropriate, in the unit.

SPECIALIST SCHOOLS

Any maintained secondary or special school, or non-maintained special school, is eligible to apply for specialist status and therefore get more funding. These then become specialist schools. They are designated in one of ten specialist areas:

- ▶ *arts*
- ▶ *business and enterprise*
- ▶ *engineering*
- ▶ *humanities*
- ▶ *language*
- ▶ *mathematics and computing*
- ▶ *music*

- ▸ *science*
- ▸ *sports*
- ▸ *technology.*

To qualify as a specialist school, a school needs to put together a four-year development plan showing how standards will be raised across the school as well as in the specialist subjects, and that they can raise sponsorship money to support their application. The law permits 10% of students to be selected by aptitude (in prescribed subjects) by schools with a specialism (this is not limited only to specialist schools).

TRUST SCHOOLS

Trust schools are funded by the government but get extra support from charitable trusts, for example an educational charity, local business or community group.

ACADEMIES (FORMERLY CITY ACADEMIES, BEFORE THE EDUCATION ACT 2002)

Academies are mixed-ability independent state schools, established and managed by independent sponsors. Core education at academies is funded by the government on the same basis as for other state schools in the locality. However, sponsors (which now include many universities) establish an endowment which is used to fund activities over and above the core education. Academies work via an Academy Trust, which is established as a charitable company, and the independent/charitable sponsor will always appoint the majority of governors. The governors are responsible for the employment of academy staff and also for admissions arrangements. Academies often appeal to parents because they are new, look good and have good facilities.

CITY TECHNOLOGY COLLEGES (CTCs)

City technology colleges are non-fee-paying schools for students over the age of 16. Their purpose is to provide vocational qualifications and A level equivalents to students which will give them practical experience and preparation for their working life. These colleges tend to be found in more urban, disadvantaged areas.

FAITH SCHOOLS

Faith schools are those which use religion as a selection criterion. Most faith schools are either voluntary controlled or voluntary aided. If voluntary controlled, they teach the locally agreed religious syllabus and the local authority is the admissions authority. If voluntary aided, the faith schools are responsible for setting their own admissions policies and teaching religious education according to their own religious beliefs.

Insight

From my experience I have noticed that more and more faith schools are being built and they are becoming extremely popular, with many being oversubscribed by their third year.

STATE SELECTIVE SCHOOLS

State selective schools can choose which kind of pupils to accept, depending on their abilities. Students are usually asked to take the 11+ exam. There are three types of selective schools:

▶ *Grammar schools – where all the students are accepted based purely on ability. These are the schools that regularly score highly in league tables.*
▶ *Partially selective schools – where some state schools take a certain number of pupils based on ability or aptitude (which can include music, singing and dancing). The majority of children however are accepted using the regular state admissions criteria.*
▶ *Banding schools – where children who wish to attend this school are tested and put into an ability band which matches their results. A certain proportion of children from each band will then be accepted into the school. The purpose of this banding is to make sure the school has a complete selection of students of all abilities.*

Understanding the importance of admissions criteria

The admissions criteria for a school form the equivalent of a job spec; if you do not meet what they are looking for, even if you have lots of other things in your favour, you will not be successful.

These criteria can change from authority to authority, school to school. They can also change from year to year.

Finding out about your preferred school's admissions criteria

It is important to research what type of school you are interested in and what its admissions criteria are. To do this, ring your local authority or check it out on the internet.

For *private schools*, the admissions criteria are usually based solely on ability: how well your child performs in the test and interview. Extra-curricular hobbies and interests may also be a factor – some schools like to accept children who will bring other, non-academic qualities/strengths that will benefit the school as a whole, such as a music or sport specialist.

The majority of *state selective schools* will base their admissions criteria on academic ability. For these types of schools there is usually a first exam (which tends to be a verbal and/or non-verbal test) where anyone wishing to sit the exam may do so. This is not always the case though, as some selective schools will only ask children to sit if they are from specific postcodes, preferring more local children to apply. After the initial test, the candidates who have scored the highest marks are invited back to sit a second examination, usually maths and English. Places are then offered based purely on the results of this test.

State selective schools may also offer music and dance within the admissions criteria; this means that pupils must meet a particular required level in these disciplines in order to be offered a place. This process is undertaken through an audition.

Most *non-selective state schools* rank their admissions criteria in the following order of priority.

1) *STATEMENTED CHILDREN*

Priority is always given to children with a statement of educational need. These children will be awarded a place at their preferred school, even if it means that the published admissions number will be exceeded.

2) *'LOOKED AFTER CHILDREN' (LAC)*

Children become 'looked after' by their local authority when their birth parents are unable to provide ongoing care in either a temporary or permanent capacity. Children can either be 'looked after' as a result of voluntary agreement by their parents or as the result of a care order. Children may be placed with kinship carers (family), network carers (extended family or friends) or foster carers, depending on individual circumstances. In 2008 there were 59,500 children 'looked after' by local authorities in England and Wales.

3) *SIBLINGS*

Children who have brothers and sisters already attending a secondary school have priority over those who do not have siblings in the school. This use of siblings within admissions criteria is commonly used by many community schools and, to a lesser extent, faith schools. This is because many LEAs believe that children in the same family should be given priority.

Warning! Remember that criteria change regularly

Before September 2008, admissions authorities could take into consideration siblings at a school in question, if they were attending the school either at the time of the application or at the time that the younger child was due to start school. However from September 2008, a sibling can only be taken into consideration if they will still be attending the school when the younger sibling starts.

Therefore, a sibling who is attending the school at the time of application but will not be at the school when the younger sibling starts will no longer be recognized as a sibling in the admissions arrangement.

4) *HOME-TO-SCHOOL DISTANCE*

The distance factor gives priority to children living closest to the school. The distance factor will be determined after applications have been received from parents and the school will allocate places according to those applicants who live nearest to it. Therefore, the admissions distance for any one school will change from year to year, depending on the volume of places requested. This means that one year you might get within the admissions area, but another year you may be outside the acceptable area, depending on the demand. It is useful to find out whether children within your postcode have been accepted in previous years. This does not guarantee you a place, but does give you an indication of possible success.

Most admission authorities will use a computer mapping programme to measure the distance between the child's home and school. Such software can measure either the shortest straight line distance or the shortest walking route.

Warning! Don't get confused!

Catchment areas and home-to-school distance are different admission criteria and authorities can use either one or the other, but not both.

5) CATCHMENT AREAS

A catchment area is a predefined area which is established *before* applications are sought from parents and it does not necessarily give priority to children living closest to the school. This is where it differs from the home-to-school distance criterion, which is defined *after* applications have been received. Here, the way the area is drawn may mean that successful applicants may not necessarily live closest to the school.

Some admission authorities use an inner and outer catchment area. In this situation priority is, first of all, given to pupils living in the inner catchment area which is usually very close to the school. If there are still places available after offering places to all those living in the inner catchment area, then pupils living in the outer catchment area are considered.

If admission authorities use catchment areas in their admissions criteria, they should provide a map of the area. This is usually included in the admissions booklet published by the local authority.

Warning! The catchment area catch!

Many parents believe that to get their child into their favourite state school, they simply need to rent or buy a property near enough to the premises to meet the catchment area/home-to-school admissions criteria for that school. In principle you may be right, but make sure you do your homework first.

▶ Check the admissions criteria for your preferred school – it might be banded or have random allocation, which means you still might not get a place for your child, even if you are living on the doorstep of this school.
▶ You need to be living in that property – it is no good buying it and renting it to others, schools will want proof that you are living at the house.

- ► *Once you have accepted a place at a school, usually in March, your place will be withdrawn at any time before the start date in September if you move to a home further away from the school.*
- ► *You may need to remain living in that home for some time after your child has started their new secondary school. This amount of time may vary from school to school but offers will be withdrawn and children will be asked to leave the school if they are not living at the premises noted on your application form.*

Expert opinion: consider home-to-school distance

'Be aware that your children have social lives! If you choose a school with a very large catchment area (they often have an extensive coach network), your son or daughter will inevitably make friends with young people who live a long way away... maybe 15, 20 miles or more. You may well spend more time than you would wish driving them here, there and everywhere at the weekends! Also remember that there will be concerts, plays, parents' evenings, sports fixtures and so on at school, and it will make a big difference to the quality of your life if you choose a school that is reasonably close to your home.'

Barbara Elliott, Head teacher of Channing School,
a private girls' secondary school in London

Don't lie about where you live!

If you lie about where you live to sneak into a school catchment area, more often than not you will be found out. Most local authorities state that if they offer a place at a school based on fraudulent or misleading information (for example a false claim about living in a catchment area), which denied a place to a child with a stronger claim, they will withdraw the offer of a place. This

(Contd)

can happen even after the child has started at their new school which would make it even more uncomfortable for them.

In order to prove that you live within the catchment area, local authorities may ask you to provide evidence in the form of utility bills, for example gas, water or electric. If they are not convinced that this is valid, they will continue to ask for proof to show that you and your family are actually living where you say you are. Therefore simply buying a property in the catchment area is not enough – you and your family need to be living there for a certain period of time. Check with your preferred school how long this needs to be.

Here's how Sheffield County Council warns their parents of fraudulent behaviour:

Fraudulent applications

'There has been a great deal of publicity – both local and national – about using false addresses to gain places at schools. The City Council makes every effort to ensure that all school places are allocated in strict accordance with its published admission arrangements. All addresses are checked with your child's primary school.

The Authority takes the issue of fraudulent application very seriously. If the Authority receives any information alleging that an application has been made fraudulently it will require parents to provide at least two forms of proof to confirm the address.

When the Authority has made an offer of a place at a school on the basis of fraudulent or intentionally misleading information, which has effectively denied a place to a child with a higher right of entry, it will be withdrawn if it comes to light before the start of the academic year. If information is received after the start of the school year that confirms a place has been obtained fraudulently, the Authority may decide not to withdraw it. Parents should note however that any subsequent application for younger children will not benefit from the sibling priority.

> If the Authority withdraws a place on the above grounds you will
> be offered a place at another school and notified of your right of
> appeal.'
>
> *Secondary Transition Guide for Parents booklet* (2009–10, page 10)

6) *SOCIAL AND MEDICAL NEEDS*

Some authorities give priority to pupils that have a social and
medical need to attend a particular school, even if they do not have
a statement of special educational needs (see Chapter 9 for more
about children with special educational needs). Social or medical
reasons would normally mean that there is a compelling need for
the child to attend a particular school and those needs cannot be
met by any other school. There is a very stringent test for these
criteria that only a very small percentage of applicants, if any, will
be able to meet. An example of such a need would be a child with a
rare medical condition who needs to be in close proximity to their
parents' home or work in case of an emergency.

Insight

In my experience it is extremely rare for school places
to be allocated using social and medical needs criteria.
Usually, if the needs are great, the child will already
have a statement and therefore will be able to choose
their school anyway.

7) *RANDOM ALLOCATION*

A very new type of admissions criterion is called random
allocation – called by some sceptics 'the lottery'. This means
that all applicants will have an equal chance of securing a place
irrespective of where they live. Brighton and Hove City Council
has become the first in the country to introduce random selection
for places at its most popular schools. (This system is used in some
parts of the US and Canada and some Scandinavian countries.)
Previously, priority in Brighton and Hove had been given to those

who lived closest. Now the city is divided into six catchment areas and pupils are expected to go to a school in their local catchment area, but not necessarily the closest one.

Where there are two schools in one catchment area, admissions are decided by lottery, not proximity. Places are allocated through an automated computer programme which is subject to independent scrutiny. All eligible school places are allocated by inputting the applicants' data into a computer and using software to produce a priority list, and the places are then allocated according to that list.

Although the system is highly divisive, supporters feel this type of admission is a fairer way to allocate places to oversubscribed schools and will prevent the practice of affluent parents in effect 'buying' a place at a popular school by moving into the school's catchment area. They believe it will widen access to schools for those unable to buy houses near to favoured schools and create greater social equality. Critics believe parents will be forced to drive their children across town, with families living close by to oversubscribed schools losing out. The debate continues.

8) *FAITH-BASED ADMISSIONS*

Schools which are designated as having a religious character (faith schools), are permitted to use faith-based admissions criteria in order to give priority to children who are members of, or who practise, their faith or denomination. This only applies if the school is oversubscribed. As part of their admission arrangements, many admission authorities require applicants to demonstrate attendance at a place of worship, often requiring a supporting statement by a religious community leader.

Parent case study

'We moved house last year in order to ensure we were living in the catchment area for a particular secondary school we wanted to send our daughters to. That was the second time we have moved home for the same reason, as we bought our last house to ensure they gained places at their current primary school. We treasure community schools as they are rare examples of where a sense of community spirit still thrives. The problem in our area of London is the exclusive nature of the intake of children at almost every school. The criteria to gain entry to most of the secondary schools where our kids' friends will most likely go are either faith-based, selective or they're private fee-paying schools.

In recent years several new faith schools opened in our area and these schools now take many of the children who would have previously attended community schools. Whilst we would not deny the right of any parent to send their children to whatever school they feel is best for them, unfortunately we do pay the price as so many children from families like ours no longer attend community schools.

So we moved within the catchment area for a community secondary school that has an excellent reputation, but is only a mile or so from where we lived before. Competition for places is so tough as the catchment area is tiny, despite the school being very large with a ten-form entry (admitting ten Year 7 classes of new pupils each year). The intake isn't really all that mixed, because the children who attend mostly live very locally and so houses in the catchment area sell for a premium, which excludes children whose family can't afford to live there. But it's perhaps the best of a bad bunch and works better for us than any other. It is true to say that if we take into account the cost of our relocation, it would have perhaps been no dearer to educate our daughters privately. I can understand why others choose that route, but we were lucky enough to have a school close by where children can gain both good grades and university places, as well as have the advantage of being part of a community school.'

Gavin, father of Lily (Year 6) and Anouska (Year 4)

9) BANDED ADMISSIONS

Some local authorities use banding as an admissions criterion to ensure that all schools have students with a wide range of ability levels. Children in Year 5 at primary school are tested and put into one of five ability groups. Parents are asked to fill in their Common Application Form and submit preferences, stating which ability band their child has been allocated. A percentage of each banded group are then offered places at these secondary schools.

Expert opinion: banding schools

'Our banding system is in place to ensure that all schools take children across all abilities. There are five bandings 1a, 1b, 2a, 2b and 3. Greenwich has a comprehensive system and this ensures that all abilities are represented at each school. One of the problems that this can cause is that the home-to-school distance can vary, according to what banding your child is in. For example, there is a school in the borough that has a specialist deaf and hearing impaired unit. Many of the band 3 places are taken up by children who have this impairment because they have special educational needs and are therefore able to request a particular school. This means that there are less band 3 places for others. If a very popular school has a lot of band 1a and 1b applicants, the home-to-school distance will shrink to reflect this. Sometimes parents don't understand why another child in their street has got into their chosen school and their child hasn't. The reason is that that child could be in another banding and the home-to-school distance is further.'

Choice Adviser for Greenwich Council, London

Questions to consider when choosing a school

WILL MY CHILD QUALIFY FOR FREE HOME-TO-SCHOOL TRANSPORT?

In the main part it's easy to find out the answer to this question as it is law! Each local authority sets out the circumstances in which a child will be provided with free home-to-school transport by using the criteria documented in the Educational Act 1996 and amended by the Education and Inspection Act 2006. The document states that, where reasonably possible and in line with government legislation, all local authorities should endeavour to offer school places within reasonable access of pupils' homes. In planning school places, local authorities should take into account the accessibility of provision in order to:

▶ *help ensure reasonable journey times for pupils*
▶ *enable as many pupils as possible to walk (or cycle) to and from school and reduce the number of car journeys in line with the authority's sustainable school travel strategy and commitment to protecting the environment.*

Therefore a pupil will typically be expected to attend the nearest suitable school at which places are available and that provides an education appropriate to their age, ability and aptitude.

If your child attends a school suggested by the local authority and the school is further than the statutory walking distance, then the local authority must make arrangements to get your child to school. The statutory walking distances is 3 miles (4.8 kilometres) for children aged eight and over.

Therefore, legally, free home-to-school transport is provided to those pupils who attend the nearest appropriate school where that school is more than three miles from their home address using the shortest available walking route. Pupils will also qualify for free home-to-school transport if they are from a low income family. The government has defined children from low income groups as those who are entitled to free school meals, or those whose families are in receipt of their maximum level of Working Tax Credit.

Thus, free transport is provided for children who are:

▶ *in receipt of free school meals or whose family is in receipt of the maximum level of Working Tax Credit*
▶ *a resident in the local authority*
▶ *aged 11–16 years and attend any of three suitable secondary schools closest to their home, where these schools are more*

than 2 miles but no more than 6 miles away or they live more
than 2 miles but no more than 15 miles away, if that is the
nearest suitable school preferred on grounds of religious belief.

Pupils not in receipt of free school meals or whose family does not receive maximum Working Tax Credit qualify for free transport if:

▶ *they are a resident in the local authority*
▶ *they are aged 8–16 years and live more than 3 miles from their nearest appropriate school.*

For all pupils, distances are measured according to the shortest available walking route. Walking distances are measured differently throughout the local authorities, some using a computerized application to calculate walking distances based on Ordnance Survey Maps, some measuring distance by the shortest available route from the nearest entrance to the home (for example, the front gate) to the nearest school entrance.

In most authorities, only about one in five secondary school students qualify for free school transport. If your child does not qualify for free travel there can be other help available for parents but you will need to check this with your local authority. For example, Plymouth City Council currently supports a concessionary fare scheme for students who are eligible for free school meals. Students who are eligible can travel to and from school for a maximum of 60p per single journey.

Warning! Free travel exceptions

There are exceptions to this rule so it is important to check with your local authority. For example, County Durham states that because it covers a wide geographical area – and consequently many students live quite a distance from their nearest school – they will provide free travel where the distance from the home address to the nearest appropriate school is more than 2 miles, rather than the usually required 3 miles, measured by the shortest available walking route.

It is important to note that pupils who have a statement of special educational needs are not automatically entitled to free transport. Each pupil will be individually assessed by their local authority according to their need. Transport may be provided where either:

▶ *the child's home-to-school distance qualifies him/her, or*
▶ *for shorter distances, where the child has an identified need that would prevent him/her walking or travelling on public transport to school.*

WILL MY CHILD QUALIFY FOR A SCHOLARSHIP OR BURSARY AT AN INDEPENDENT SCHOOL?

Many private schools offer scholarships or bursaries to help families who would not be able to afford the school fees. Most scholarships are offered solely on outstanding academic performance of the child – those who come top in their exams or display a particular talent. No additional examinations are set for these academic awards and it is not necessary to apply for them as they will be offered by the school automatically if they feel it is appropriate. Specialist scholarships, for example in music, are applied for in advance and your child will be asked to sit an additional test based on your child's aptitude in this specialist area. The size of the scholarship, sometimes known as an 'exhibition', varies depending on the calibre of the individual child and how much the school wants them. Top scholarships usually go up to 50% of the school fees, but more common offers are between 15 and 25%. It is important to note that children applying for musical scholarships at private schools must have passed the entrance examination first.

Insight
In my experience it is often the case that the same child is offered scholarships by a range of schools.

If you wish to apply for a bursary, your child will still have to show academic talent. Bursaries can cover anything from 10–100% of the school fees. You will be asked to fill in a form which will require giving information about your family's financial circumstances – a form of means testing – based on:

- *income*
- *pensions*
- *tax and national insurance paid out*
- *any rent or mortgage that is paid*
- *the value of your property*
- *other assets, savings and capital liabilities.*

This is required to ensure that support is provided to those with the greatest need. Schools will consider each case on its own merits taking into account the total family income and assets and liabilities. Schools say they aim to be as sensitive and flexible as possible in allocating the finite funds they have. There is usually a maximum level set for each school with regards to a family yearly income, above which a bursary would not be considered. This level varies from school to school so it is important to find out what this level is before filling in the form. Most schools review their bursaries annually and a change in family circumstances will often result in a change to the amount of assistance that can be provided.

In addition, support is often available for extra-curricular activities that benefit a student's education, for example academic trips.

Expert opinion: bursaries

'No one would pretend that the financial demands of an independent education are trivial. Whether your preference is for boarding or day school, the overall outlay on a full private secondary education is likely to be many tens of thousands of pounds. Understandably, there are relatively few parents who do not have to consider the financial implications extremely carefully and many are deterred altogether. And yet, there may be help at hand.

The vast majority of independent schools are registered charities with a very long and generous history of providing bursaries and fee assistance to those who might otherwise not be able to benefit.

In the wake of the Charities Act 2006, which removed the automatic presumption that educational charities operate for the public benefit, an increasing number of independent schools are seeking to restate their inclusivity by offering means-tested bursaries. Typically, such fee assistance is offered as a percentage remission of the total tuition fees charged each term and, depending upon the assessed need and the resources the school has available, can range right up to 100% in some cases. It is important to remember that there are no standardized criteria for means testing but schools will tend to use an assessment that reflects both their ability to give and the catchment they serve.

Before discussing how to apply for a bursary, it goes without saying that you should first choose a school that will otherwise meet the needs of your child. Schools will certainly look at things from that perspective and are extremely unlikely to even begin to consider fee assistance until they have decided which applicants are suitable pupils for their particular setting. In other words they will conduct an entry selection process based on the child's abilities and potential and not upon the parents' ability to pay fees. Only when they have decided who to offer places to will they consider the allocation of whatever bursary funding they have to offer. Here, the reality is that few, if any, schools yet have the ability to operate 'needs blind', regardless of parental ability to pay fees. The offer of a place will therefore not necessarily be a guarantee that bursary funding is available.

So, what about applying? The school website is often a good place to start but the school prospectus will usually make it clear what fee assistance might be available and how it should be applied for. Usually, you will be asked to submit full and considerable detail about your income and outgoings, your assets and liabilities. You may feel uncomfortable about this, but remember that the school will be very experienced at dealing with bursary applications in a sensitive, professional and entirely discreet manner. Very few people indeed will ever know who has applied for fee assistance, or who receives it, least of all the pupils.

(Contd)

However, the school does need to have the information it asks for and the most important thing is to be open, clear and honest. Schools will usually validate means testing data on an annual basis and attempts to misrepresent or mislead are unlikely to go undetected and will inevitably rebound. Remember that you will be judged by exactly the same criteria as everyone else who applies to your chosen school and if you do not apply then you will not get anything.'

Jeremy Witts, Director of Finance and Administration, University College School, a private boys' secondary school in London

Get ready – a checklist of what to do in the years leading up to secondary transfer

YEAR 3 (CHILD'S AGE: 7–8)

For many schools this is the first stage of the juniors and for every child the beginning of key stage 2. This is often a 'settling in' year for both teachers and parents.

Things to do
1 *Start doing your homework. Check to see what secondary schools you have in your area and what their admissions criteria are. Think about the different types of schools and whether you will be considering private or state. If thinking about private, it is important to get a realistic idea of how much it will cost. Don't forget to include uniform, lunches, equipment and school trips… it all adds up.*
2 *Start considering if you would like your child to learn a musical instrument or start a particular hobby. What is your child interested in? What do they have a natural flair for? What qualities might their future secondary school value most?*

YEAR 4 (CHILD'S AGE: 8–9)

This is the year in which teachers encourage children to become increasingly independent and some parents begin to think about tutors.

Things to do

1 *Encourage your child to join clubs inside and outside of their primary school. If your child is interested in music, get them started on an instrument early; by the time they get to secondary transfer they might be in a good position for a specialist school, a selective state based on music or a private school.*

2 *If considering a religious secondary school you might want to start regularly attending houses of worship, if appropriate.*

3 *Start thinking about possible tutors for 11+ examinations for both state selective and private schools. Good tutors have long waiting lists!*

4 *Ask class teachers the ability level of your child and the type of secondary school you should be considering. Teachers will already be making long-term judgements on your child and will have a good idea of the National Curriculum level they are working at based on their teacher assessments. Remember to ask for feedback on recent test results: most schools perform end-of-year optional Qualifications and Curriculum Authority (QCA) tests, which are like mini-SATs and give a good indication of how children are performing against the national average. Many schools tend not to volunteer this information unless specifically asked by parents for it.*

Insight

Over the last few years, primary head teachers have started to invite Year 3 and 4 parents to secondary transition meetings as they are aware that this process can be stressful and parents are increasingly wanting information earlier.

YEAR 5 (CHILD'S AGE: 9–10)

This is the year when the pace increases and the gossip about secondary school starts to bubble up.

Things to do

1 *Visit secondary schools. Many state schools only invite Year 6 parents and students to attend open days, but on entering they don't ask for your child's birth certificate! By Year 6 you will*

only have a couple of months to decide as most open days are in September with completed Common Application Forms (CAF) being handed in for October so it is useful to visit a year ahead of time.

2   *Consider whether your child will qualify for free home-to-school transport as this may affect your choice of schools.*

3   *Arrange a meeting with your child's head teacher to discuss secondary school options. Again, try to get a realistic idea of your child's ability; you do not want to be entering them for state selective or private entrance exams if they do not stand a chance.*

4   *Recruit the services of a tutor. It is important to bear in mind the purpose of the tutor; it is not to help improve your child's ability but simply to familiarize your child with the type of questions they will be asked in the examinations and teach them helpful ways of showing their work in the best light. If your child is 'over-tutored' to pass the exams, when they start the school they will be unhappy. Make sure you are tutoring for the right reasons.*

5   *If appropriate, start thinking about whether you would qualify for scholarships or bursaries at private schools.*

YEAR 6 (CHILD'S AGE: 10–11)

This is SATs year, the year when pupils sit end-of-key stage 2 examinations and – for the majority of students – the last year of primary school.

Things to do

1   *Revisit favoured secondary schools. Details to do with transition can change year to year, including admissions criteria, so it is very useful repeating a visit. NEVER ASSUME THINGS WILL BE THE SAME AS LAST YEAR.*

2   *Fill in your local authority secondary school Common Application Form (CAF), checking beforehand that your child meets the admissions criteria for your chosen preferred schools.*

3   *Fill in any additional application forms which may be required by your chosen secondary schools.*

4 *Be ready to appeal in March if you feel you have a case.*
5 *Prepare your child for the differences they will experience
in secondary school.*

Parent case study

'My eldest child Adam is now in Year 6 and the whole secondary process
has been new and bewildering to say the least. For years you casually
discuss the various school options but before you know it the whole
process is upon you!

Adam began being tutored in Year 4. After asking several other parents at
the school for contacts for good tutors, only one mother was prepared
and happy to give out an actual phone number! Suddenly, parents became
secretive and highly competitive. Each claimed that their child hadn't
started being tutored yet, but by the end of Year 4, most of the children in
my son's year confessed to "having a tutor and lots of homework!"

As Adam entered Year 5, the pressure started to build up. The "exam"
word was being mentioned at school more often and the workload was
beginning to mount. One kind parent with an older child, advised us to
attend secondary school open evenings that year, to avoid a mad dash
in Year 6.

This was great advice as so many of the schools overlap on the same
evening and we therefore managed to pace ourselves over two school
years and view many different schools.

At my son's school, a meeting was held for Year 5 and Year 6 parents
to explain and discuss the secondary transfer process and the
options available. This meeting was very helpful as it clarified all the
outstanding questions and many of the myths that you hear during
the process. After seeing and selecting certain schools with your child,
the next stage is to fill in each school's application form and then
finally complete your local authority form. I was extremely careful and
thorough after hearing how a friend the year before had forgotten to
send her local authority form in and therefore was not entitled to a

(Contd)

place at their "excellent local secondary school". A mistake easily done! You soon realize that you must ensure that all forms are sent back by their due date and visit each school and do not go by hearsay!

Throughout the past two school years, I have been actively involved in Adam's school and tutor work. I time his work regularly and keep a check with his school teachers and tutor on his progress and weaknesses. I have invested in many exam papers and revision books and ensure that he has worked thoroughly and at a steady pace. Adam was also read widely, compiling a list of authors that he enjoyed, and over the past years, he has built up a library at home to be proud of.

As a novice to this whole system, I have found it to be exhausting, at times confusing and often frustrating. I feel I have become an expert on the subject of secondary transfer having had to scurry around and gather information by myself. Next time around, I will be far wiser, more relaxed and more knowledgeable on the subject. I pity those parents in years to come with their eldest child at this stage. For now, I can sit back and be thankful that my youngest son is in Year 2!'

Debra, mother of Adam (Year 6)

Frequently asked questions

WHICH IS BETTER: SINGLE-SEX SCHOOLS OR MIXED-SEX SCHOOLS?

The debate is ongoing. Many people believe that girls and boys need to be educated separately. They believe that the opposite sex can act as a negative distraction with more worrying about appearance and less about academic matters, and a greater focus on social life rather than school life.

Many believe that boys and girls learn differently and that certain teaching styles are better suited to one sex than the other: for example, boys appear to do better when they learn in a kinaesthetic, practical and 'making' environment.

A disadvantage with single-sex schools is that some children may see the opposite sex as something unusual and unattainable – not the kind of people you are around every day. There are many entrenched views on this subject and the debate will continue but the current trend shows a clear decline in the number of single-sex schools. You should just consider the needs of your own child and decide which environment will suit them better.

WILL MY CHILD LEARN MORE AT A SMALLER RATHER THAN A LARGER SCHOOL?

As always there are advantages and disadvantages to schools of all sizes. Your child may feel lost in a large school or suffocated in a smaller school. Your child's personality should play a key role in deciding whether they would prefer to be a small fish in a large pond or a large fish in a small pond.

HOW USUAL IS IT FOR PRIVATE SCHOOLS TO OFFER BURSARIES OR SCHOLARSHIPS?

While the amount of financial support will vary, schools will offer this type of support to students each year. Over half a million students are educated in schools represented by the Independent Schools Council (ISC). More than one in three of these students at ISC schools receive assistance with fees with four out of five of these awards coming directly from the school itself.

How to prepare the ground for secondary transfer

▶ *Research the different types of schools early – don't leave it until Year 6. If you find out that due to the admissions criteria you do not have a realistic chance of success, it is far better dealing with the disappointment early, giving you time to reconsider your choices.*

(Contd)

- ▶ After deciding on the type of school you would like, encourage your child to take up the extra-curricular hobbies that will make their future applications stronger.
- ▶ Make sure you are fully aware of the admissions procedure for the different types of schools and don't assume that it will stay the same for when your child is in Year 6.
- ▶ Think about how your child will journey to secondary school. Ask yourself the following questions:
  - ▷ Can your child walk to the school and what might that journey be like in the winter?
  - ▷ Are there other children nearby that your child could walk to school with?
  - ▷ Can they cycle to school and does the school have bicycle storage facilities?
  - ▷ Do you know the fares you might expect to pay on a daily, monthly and yearly basis?
  - ▷ How realistic would it be to take your child to school by car, and what if there are days when you can't?
  - ▷ What option gives you flexibility when your child joins after-school clubs?
- ▶ If you are looking for a religious school, make sure in advance that you are following all the recommended practices and procedures.
- ▶ If thinking about relocating to be near the school of your choice, check that home-to-school distance is a major criterion. For state selective schools you could live next door but still not be successful as your child will only be judged based on academic performance. The same may be true for faith schools.
- ▶ If needed, book a tutor early. Good tutors always have long waiting lists.
- ▶ Try to get as much information as you can from your child's primary school about your child's ability level so you have realistic expectations from which to make the right secondary school choices.

10 THINGS TO REMEMBER

1 *There are two main types of schools available at secondary level – private and state.*

2 *Private schools charge a fee and entrance to them is usually through an examination and interview.*

3 *State schools are free and are usually run by the local authority.*

4 *All children are welcome to apply to state schools. However, if a school is oversubscribed then priority will be given to those who meet their admissions criteria.*

5 *Admissions criteria can change from year to year so regular checking is essential.*

6 *It is important to consider secondary school choices well ahead of time.*

7 *State selective schools are state schools where the main admissions criteria are either aptitude or musical talent. Examinations and/or auditions are required for entry into these schools.*

8 *Priority for entry into state schools is given to children who are looked after by their local authority or who have statements of special educational needs.*

9 *Scholarships are offered to children who have sat exams for entry into the private sector. A child does not apply for a scholarship – it will be offered by the school if they feel it is appropriate.*

10 *Bursaries to private schools need to be requested ahead of a child sitting an exam.*

3

How to shortlist the right school for your child

In this chapter you will learn:
- *how to find out more about schools in your area*
- *how to interpret key documents – league tables, Ofsted inspection reports, a school prospectus – and 'word of mouth' information*
- *about the school visit.*

Technology makes it simple and fast for you not only to identify possible schools for your children but to form strong opinions about them before you even set foot inside them. This is done by surfing the net – using websites wisely and gathering as much information as you can. Here's how to start.

Sources of information about secondary schools

The following is a list of sources of information for finding out about secondary schools. We'll look at each one in detail, and how to interpret them.

- ▶ *government and local education authority websites*
- ▶ *Choice Advisers*

- *school prospectus, website and profile*
- *Ofsted website*
- *league tables*
- *'word of mouth'*
- *school visit and/or open day.*

Government and local education authority websites

The first website to check should be the government website www.direct.gov.uk. This is the official government website for all UK citizens. Click on the 'education and learning' heading and then to the 'schools section' which includes 'choosing a school' as an option, and which contains lots of useful background information such as admissions criteria and details of how to apply to each school.

Your local education authority's (LEA) website will tell you how the schooling system works in your area. This differs from authority to authority: some have infants, junior and secondary schools systems, some have first, middle and upper school systems. The age at which your child transfers to secondary school will be governed by which school system your borough has in place.

To access your local authority site you can put their name in a search engine, for example 'Bristol local authority' or 'Bristol City Council'. A home page telling you about all the services offered by this authority will come up on screen; you then need to navigate yourself to the education section, then to secondary schools and then finally to the schools' admission pages. This will vary from site to site, but generally all local authorities will have the details of their approach to secondary transfer detailed on their website.

Insight

I found it useful researching local schools by simply putting 'Barnet Secondary Schools' into a search engine. This signposted me to all the websites that could help me.

It is important to remember that while most local authorities transfer their children to secondary school at the end of Year 6, some do it at other times. Find out ahead of time the situation for your local authority as this may significantly influence your decisions.

Parent case study

'Throughout the UK, children finish their primary school at the end of Year 6 and start secondary school in Year 7. As far as I am aware, possibly one of the few exceptions to this is the London Borough of Harrow, where I live. Here they transfer at the end of Year 7.

This is currently being reviewed by the authority, and may change in the foreseeable future, but my view is that the secondary school is set up to teach in a completely different way. French is three times a week and not once, there are woodwork facilities, AstroTurf pitches, proper science labs and English is formally divided into language and literature. Add to this the fact the children have to grow up and learn to ensure they have all the correct books, manage their homework and take more responsibility and I felt it would put my twin boys at a disadvantage to do this a year later than most other children. For this reason I had no choice but to look for a school outside my borough and ask my sons to sit the entrance exams. This is because they would not have been accepted by other non-selective schools out of the borough, as we did not meet their admissions criteria – usually catchment area.

For me, this was an extremely stressful time as I was looking for two places and not one. With pressure from parents inside catchment areas, it is becoming increasingly difficult to get any child into a school outside the borough. The numbers of places being offered are getting less and the number of children applying is increasing. We were very fortunate insofar as both my boys were lucky enough to get into our first choice school. But things don't stay the same. My boys started at their new school in September 2008 and already the sibling criteria have changed. We live too far away for the sibling policy to be valid, so in 2011 we will be doing all this again for my other son – it will probably be harder and definitely be just as stressful, but like many parents there is no alternative.'

Karoline, mother of David and Andrew (Year 7)

Choice Advisers

Some LEAs offer parents helplines or Choice Advisers. It is worth giving them a call – a human voice can be so much warmer and more helpful than a computer screen. Choice Advisers provide free one-to-one advice to families who are at the point of making an application for a place in a Reception class or for a Year 7 place at secondary school. Choice Advisers provide information and support to help parents complete the admissions process and they provide realistic and impartial information about schools. Their job includes:

- *explaining things if you are having difficulties*
- *answering any questions and concerns you may have*
- *helping you understand and fill in paperwork and online forms for local and out-of-area schools*
- *providing independent, realistic and impartial information about maintained schools in your area, including:*
  - ▷ *the admissions policy*
  - ▷ *how likely you are to get a place*
  - ▷ *the school's Ofsted report*
  - ▷ *the school's performance, value-added data and exam results*
  - ▷ *the school's specialist or academy status*
  - ▷ *explaining the school prospectus*
  - ▷ *the school's special needs policy and provision*
  - ▷ *term times, school hours, uniform requirement*
  - ▷ *information about transport to and from school*
- *providing contact details for other schools so you can make contact if you wish*
- *supporting you through the appeals process*
- *providing contacts for other services you may find useful.*

Advice and support is available for all parents/carers applying for a primary or secondary school place. However, Choice Advisers are particularly keen to support:

- *parents/carers and children who need help to understand the admissions process*

- *parents/carers of a child looked after by the local authority*
- *parents who find it difficult asking for help at their child's primary school*
- *parents/carers who may need support with reading and/or writing*
- *families with English as a second language*
- *families that have recently arrived in the UK*
- *parents/carers of children who are not currently in school*
- *families living in difficult circumstances.*

Insight

While researching for this book, I realized that Choice Advisers are not very well marketed and many parents are not aware of their existence. It's worth your while asking to talk to one – they really know their stuff!

Expert opinion: Choice Adviser

'Parents of children going from Year 6 to Year 7 now have more choice than ever before of the school their child will go to. However, with choice comes a need to spend time and effort choosing, and a responsibility for that choice. "How much easier it was when children went to the school down the road," I am often told. Easier, yes, but the best school for your child?

In Bristol we have a great variety of state secondary schools (as well as independent schools). We have seven academies benefiting from sponsors that bring not only money and equipment to the school but also their expertise. We have a trust school consisting of a nursery, primary, special school, secondary school and college. All of these are on the same campus where children can be educated from the ages of 0–19. There are extended schools which also provide care outside of school hours and community schools which work closely with local communities to the benefit of both the school and the community.

Are we surprised then that parents are finding it increasingly harder to make their choices? Once they have got to grips with the different types of schools they then have to unravel the application process and understand the oversubscription criteria in order to make their choices realistic. Whilst everyone has a choice, there has to be a way of making allocation fair and applying the oversubscription criteria to the most popular schools makes the allocation process open and clear. It is pointless applying for a school that is traditionally oversubscribed if you live the other side of the city and have no brothers or sisters at the school. When making choices you have to take the criteria into account and use the laws of probability to rule out some and to include others. I am often approached by parents who want to apply to the three most popular schools but do not meet any of the criteria and consequently are unlikely to be allocated any of them but may be allocated one that they would not want to go to. Convincing them to make at least one realistic choice that they are happy with is not easy until they understand all the facts and the processes. Getting them to go and look at some of the more realistic choices has often been an eye opener to them when they realize that there are other good schools out there that meet their needs other than those three 'most popular schools'. Usually they are happy to keep one or two 'dream schools' (that they may have little chance of getting) whilst including one or two schools that, having researched them a bit more, they could be happy with.

Having chosen their three schools, the next confusion – not helped by some head teachers who tell parents "You must put our school first or you will not get a place in this school" – arises as they try to put schools in order of preference. Parents strive to put their dream school first but in doing so are afraid they will lose the chance of a place at their local school. A common question is: "If I put school 'A' as third choice does that mean they will not consider me because it will be full up by the time they get to third choices?" A loud sigh of relief is heard as I explain 'equal preference', which means that all schools applied for are considered equally, with the order of

(Contd)

preference only coming into play if more than one of their choices are able to be offered.

As a Choice Adviser in Bristol, I feel privileged that I am able to talk to parents throughout Bristol – in primary schools or individually – to give them information on the different types of schools available to them and why some schools may suit a child better than another school. Giving them the information they need in easy language and having time to answer their questions has been a life saver to many parents who have used the Choice Advice service. Although it does not seem like it to parents who sometimes see an unfairness in the allocation of schools, all we want, both parents and local authority, is to have a happy, contented child at school. My advice is to spend as much time as you can to find out about schools, to visit schools whilst the pupils are there and get your questions and concerns answered. Then use the oversubscription criteria to make realistic choices.

A child that attends a school that has been chosen wisely, with an informed decision made for that particular child, is more likely to attend school, to be happy at school and to succeed at school… that is surely what we all want for our young people?'

Denise Tovey, Choice Adviser for Bristol City Council

School prospectus, website and profile

When you have identified a school of interest you can research them further by looking at their own website. You can also telephone them and ask them for a school prospectus. Some schools allow you to download their prospectus online.

The school prospectus will tell you a lot of information about the school – typically their values, facilities, curriculum range, links with the community and leadership – and usually opens with a welcome from the head teacher. It may also include GCSE and

A level results and university places secured by current Year 13 leavers.

The school profile is an annual report for parents, written by the school itself, which contains information about the school. School profiles can be read online at http://schoolsfinder.direct.gov.uk/. The profile will tell you what has been successful in the last year, what the school has improved at, how much the children have made progress over time and how the school accommodates the needs of all of their children. The report also includes a school performance summary and children's results at different key stages.

Don't be fooled by the glossy cover, photographs of happy children and positive spin on school websites, prospectuses or profiles. Remember it is written by the school to sell itself to parents and will be only highlighting their strengths and not discussing their weaknesses. Looking at the school profile will be very helpful if the school you have in mind has not undergone a recent Ofsted inspection.

Expert opinion: choosing a school

'One question parents very rarely ask when they visit a school is what is its marketing or advertising budget. Why is it a valid question? It's stressful enough choosing a school for one's child anyway, but what many parents have seen or read that has drawn them to a particular school has not been produced by those who will teach your child, or even by educators. Rather, it will have been produced by highly-paid marketing people and designers whose job it is to sell you the "product", and not to decide whether they would send their own children there.

It's worth remembering one definition of marketing: "... the art of selling you something you didn't know you needed". Books such as this are important precisely because they have no vested interest behind them and are truly independent. Their freedom is to show you, the parent, the simplest paths on the long and demanding journey to

(Contd)

choosing a secondary school, and to let you shine a torch in to areas the marketing people would sometimes prefer you not to see.

Yet with all this there comes one basic truth about choosing a school. It's a bit like being shown round a house by an estate agent. You have some idea of what it is you want, but you see house after house that doesn't do it for you. Then, all of a sudden, WHAM! It's "IA" (instant appeal), and from that moment on, that's the house you want. One very distinguished head teacher always used to say that 55 minutes of the hour she insisted on spending with every prospective parent was a complete waste of time, undertaken to reassure her rather than the parents. The parents knew within five minutes if this was what they wanted to be *their* school. There's no mystery about how it happens. Every parent knows, even if only subconsciously, three things. They know their child even better than perhaps the child knows itself. They know roughly what they want from a school, ranging from "results-results-results-and-a-place-at-Oxford-now" at one extreme end of the spectrum to "I-don't-care-if-he-fails-everything-I-just-want-him-to-be-happy" at the other. And thirdly, as adults, they've seen a few things and done a few things, and take in all the little signs – smiling faces, clean loos, no graffiti – that tell them whether a school is happily and well run or not. These three items are like the loose bits of a jigsaw. Find the right school and suddenly they all click into place. Use your head in choosing a school, and read books like this. But most of all when choice time comes use your heart and back your hunch and "IA".'

Jenny Stephen, Headmistress of South Hampstead High School,
a private girls' school in London

Ofsted website

A useful source of unbiased information about a school can come from Ofsted. Ofsted (Office for Standards in Education, Children's Services and Skills) is the government department that inspects and regulates institutions in England providing education to learners of all ages and providers of care for children and young people.

To access Ofsted reports from your local schools you will need to log onto the Ofsted website, www.ofsted.gov.uk. Click on 'inspection reports', choose the type of school you are interested in, and type in your postcode. All the recent reports for schools in your area will come up. Make sure you check the date of the report – they can quickly go out of date. Also note that new schools tend to be inspected for the first time in their second year; inspections in the first year are extremely rare.

Ofsted inspections are constantly changing. It is worth noting that the length of time between inspections can change too. Judgements made and the scoring structures also change over time, but the main points to look at are the range of scores possible for any given Ofsted and what the school scored related to this range.

So what do Ofsted judge? Ofsted will look at the overall effectiveness of the school, including the quality of:

▶ *teaching and learning*
▶ *curriculum and other activities offered by the school*
▶ *pastoral care, guidance and support*
▶ *behaviour management*
▶ *management and leadership.*

Private schools have Ofsted-type inspections too. These are carried out by the Independent Schools Council (ISC) who have their own inspectorate. It is worth noting that private schools who are not members of ISC will have their Ofsted carried out by the same inspectors as the state sector.

INTERPRETING OFSTED INSPECTION REPORTS

Ofsted reports usually give an accurate picture of a school and if it is judged to be outstanding or good then it is certainly worth looking at. Caution needs to be taken with schools in special measures – that means that it has serious shortcomings and the inspectors are considering closing it down. Look at the students' own judgements about the school and also Ofsted's letter back to students – it is a great device for cutting through the jargon and hearing what the inspectors really think about the school. Having interviewed many parents it is my understanding that discipline is a major deciding factor for parents and Ofsted reports will comment on this. Be suspicious if a report includes phrases like 'low level of disruption' or 'a few are too boisterous at break' or 'find it difficult to sit still and listen in class'.

Insight

In my experience the success of a school can change quite dramatically with a new head teacher and senior management team at the helm. Therefore, you might find it helpful to check how long a head has been in place since the last Ofsted as you could find that the report is rather outdated.

Did you know?

The Welsh equivalent of Ofsted is called Estyn. Estyn is the office of Her Majesty's Inspectorate for Education and Training in Wales. It is independent of, but funded by, the National Assembly for Wales under Section 104 of the Government of Wales Act 1998.

In Scotland, HM Inspectorate of Education (HMIE) assumes this role. It has responsibilities to evaluate the quality of pre-school education, all schools, teacher education, community learning and development, further education and local authorities.

League tables

League tables were introduced in 1992 to give parents guidance when it comes to choosing a school for their child. Although tables are no longer published in Scotland, Wales and Northern Ireland, their use has continued in England.

INTERPRETING LEAGUE TABLES: WHAT MATTERS AND WHAT DOESN'T

The league table debate is ongoing, with many people outraged that exam results are used to measure the success of a school. League tables measure the academic results of children who sit tests – but many believe this is not necessarily a fair measure of the performance of a school. For this you need to take into consideration a number of other factors, including the 'value-added' measure, the number of children with EAL (English as an additional language), student turnover and the number of children with special needs. All of these factors will affect a school's results and may lead to poorer standing in the tables. Therefore my advice is: look at the tables, but consider other factors as well. The quality of pastoral care within a school is a very important factor and sadly there is no league table for this.

When you are looking at tables for secondary schools be aware that GCSE results are displayed in two ways: A*–C grades and A*–G grades. Pay closer attention to the former; it is a better reflection on the success of the students. Also look at the range of subjects covered at GCSE level; the better schools encourage their students to take more challenging GCSEs. It is also useful to examine which university places are taken up by Year 13 leavers; this can give helpful insight into the success of a school.

To access up-to-date league table information you can check the following websites: www.dfes.gov.uk/performancetables/ or http://news.bbc.co.uk/1/hi/education/league_tables/default.stm.

'Word of mouth'

Personal recommendations are always useful. Whether it is for a home help, a babysitter, a carpenter or car mechanic, you will feel easier if someone else has used them and is happy with their service. The same can be said about schools. If you know of other children who have had positive experiences in particular schools it will make you more likely to want to send your child there. Equally, if parents and children are constantly criticizing a school, you will most likely be put off it.

INTERPRETING 'WORD OF MOUTH'

It is important to make sure that you get an objective view about a school as well because parents' views are often not reliable. Some may be overly devoted to a school, others overly critical for personal reasons which would not necessarily be relevant to your child. Equally, every child is different and a school that suits one child does not necessarily suit another. Remember too that schools are subject to change. Don't make up your mind based on past glories.

Questions to ask parents 'in the know'

▶ Is your child happy at the school?
▶ Does your child enjoy learning and feel the amount of homework is fair?
▶ What are the school's strengths?
▶ What are the school's weaknesses?
▶ How well does the school communicate with parents?
▶ Does the school have any problems with behaviour?
▶ Did your child find it easy to transfer from primary school?
▶ How well has your child integrated with others in their class or year group?

It is a good idea to not only ask the parents, but ask the children these questions too. Accessing the mind of a teenager can be an adventure in itself and never assume you know what makes them tick.

Expert opinion: choosing the right school

'The choice of secondary school can be one of the most important decisions that a parent will take for their child – or, more likely in this day and age, *with* their child. For those who are coming to such a decision for the first time it can be a daunting prospect.

In making this choice, whilst statistics and league tables can be useful starting points, it is important that parents go beyond these and focus on the talents, needs and personality of their child. They need to look for the type of establishment that would best suit those needs and then set out to find that school. It may well be (it almost certainly should be) that it is the values and beliefs of an institution that help parents finally to decide which school is most appropriate rather than any bald facts and figures.

To visit a number of schools is, of course, vital – even if the first school seems to be the 'one' – and it is best to do this with son and daughter in tow. Open days are fine to get a feel for the potential choice but, if the opportunity is there to visit it during a 'normal' working day, then it is important to take it – to see what the school is really like when it is not trying to sell itself. It is essential, too, to look at the physical environment and to find out whether the school will be able to cater for any special talents or learning needs that a child might have.

To meet with the head teacher is always desirable. He/she will set the tone for the school and it is important that parents (and child) feel comfortable with what he/she has to say and that there are shared views about the educational focus and direction of the school. Conversations with pupils and parents (a good school will provide contact details) will quickly confirm whether an individual will fit in easily and make friends quickly.

It is important that the final choice is a shared one and that the younger opinions are taken into consideration. Remember, though, that this is a decision for the long term and the ten-year-old view is inevitably framed in a timescale that is much shorter; whatever they say, new friends will easily be made.

(Contd)

School visit and/or open day

First impressions are very important. Just like buying a new house, you will get an immediate feel for a school. You will make judgements about the external architecture, the behaviour of the children and the pastoral care of the staff. Take time to weigh up all the different aspects of the school before making important decisions.

Insight

When I went visiting schools I took my husband with me first of all, then if we liked it we went back with our daughter. I didn't want her to set her heart on a school that we felt wasn't right for her.

What to look for at school visits

- Do the children interact well with their teachers?
- How at ease is the head teacher with the children – does he/she know their names?
- Are any teachers shouting?
- Are the students getting on with the task and busy working independently?
- Are the students proud of their school?
- Are the premises well maintained and safe – is there any graffiti?
- Is there a high standard of general cleanliness of furniture, desks, walls and so on?

- Are the students' books marked with constructive comments and suggestions for improvement?
- Are the children given targets?
- Does the school offer a wide variety of extra-curricular activities?
- Do the classrooms look bright and cheery? Are the displays recent and are pieces of work displayed from all children, not just the most able with the neatest handwriting?
- Does the head teacher appear to be a good leader, giving you a clear understanding of the school's aims and ethos?

Try to visit during a school day to get an accurate reflection of a typical day. Many schools offer visits after school or during an open day but it is not the same as a normal school day. If you can, try to pop into one of the children's toilets – it can tell you a lot about the school – and might tell you some school gossip as well! Find out where most of the students live and how they journey to school – at secondary school your child will want to be able to travel to school independently.

Questions to ask staff at school visits

- Would you send your child to this school?
- What is the number of applications per place? Is the school oversubscribed?
- How do you deal with bullying? Have you ever excluded or expelled a child?
- Is discipline a problem at this school?
- What is the staff and student turnover?
- How many members of staff are supply teachers?
- What are the strengths and weaknesses of the school?
- What are the class sizes? How are they organized?
- What is the cultural/religious mix of the school? How is this reflected in the curriculum?

(Contd)

- ▶ Does the school have any special resources – for example, a photography room?
- ▶ Is there an after-school or homework club?
- ▶ Is there an active parent/teacher association?
- ▶ What percentage of children stays on in the sixth form? What universities do they get into and what do they study?
- ▶ What is your student exclusion rate?

Questions to ask students at school visits

- ▶ Are you happy here?
- ▶ What happens if you misbehave?
- ▶ What are the best and worst things about this school?
- ▶ Have you ever had to deal with bullying?
- ▶ How do you travel to and from school?

It is easy to be impressed by excellent grounds and facilities for sports, music, drama or art, but try to stay focused on what is important for the development of your own child's needs when choosing a school. Some children thrive in a more formally structured environment while others prefer a less formal atmosphere. Schools have different styles and it is important to choose one where your child feels comfortable and which gives them appropriate motivation.

Expert opinion: selective secondary schools

'With regard to entry to selective secondary schools, the same rules apply that apply to all schools. You need to choose a school based on how well you think it will suit your child and to make this judgement you need to get to know the school by reading about it, visiting it, speaking to pupils and getting to know its particular entrance requirements and procedures. All this should be possible through a visit to a school open afternoon or evening.

A good school will listen to its pupils and have a strong conviction about its educational purpose and the importance of helping all pupils to succeed. You should also be able to see examples of its approach and ethos in all areas of the school – in the pupils, the displays and the teachers.'

Oliver Blond, Head teacher of The Henrietta Barnett School,

a girls' state selective secondary school in North London

Frequently asked questions

Should I wait until my child is in Year 6 before I visit secondary schools?
No. Private schools welcome visits from parents of children of any age and while some state schools sometimes urge only Year 6 parents to attend open days, this is due to fears about large numbers attending on the day. Don't worry though, they won't frisk you at the door and check the age of your child!

My friend's child goes to a local secondary school and is very unhappy; should this put me off sending my child there?
Possibly yes, possibly no. It depends on why your friend's child is unhappy. It may be because of very specific reasons that will not be relevant to your child, and therefore you should not consider this in your decision-making process. If, however, the child is unhappy due to more general issues then you should certainly take these into account, investigate further and possibly address these issues directly with the school.

Friends tell me not to worry about league tables; are they right?
League tables are a very useful source of information about a school. However, they must not be used in isolation. There are a number of factors that can make a high impact on scores such as number of children with English as an additional language or

number of children with special needs. These will affect the league table scores but will not be an indication of the success of a school.

Should I be put off if there is a lot of graffiti around a school's premises?

Graffiti, or similar signs such as broken walls or run-down gardens do give an indication of neglect of the school premises and possible lack of respect that students have for their surroundings. Nonetheless, this should not be used as a sole measure of the school – other pointers such as the attitude and behaviour of the students you meet at a visit, the league table score and the Ofsted report should also be used to gain an overall picture of the success of a school.

Should I choose the local school as I know my child will hate to travel?

Travelling independently to and from school is very much a part of the transition from primary to secondary school and many children like this newfound independence. Some enjoy taking public transport or school buses and use this time to bond with friends and see it as an integral social part of the day. Don't take things for granted; discuss with your child how they feel about it.

Expert opinion: go with your gut feeling

'"The heart, not head" is the single most important factor; happiness is the key to total education and to all successful learning. You and your child will feel whether the environment is right and conducive, and feel that within minutes; the rest is all confirmation.

Never forget that schools are about people and personal relationships, they are about a sense of community and well-being, about genuine excitement in learning and extra-curricular activity, not about facilities or systems or tables. Do not be misled by crude tables, but rather ask what former pupils have done, which universities they study at and career paths they follow; check how many get their desired course at their first choice university.

Talk to current and former parents and pupils. Talk to teaching staff as well as support staff. Visit on an open day and on a working day and talk to pupils in and out of their lessons. Watch lesson changeovers and break times. Get a sense of pupil–pupil interaction, pupil–teacher interaction, teacher–teacher interaction and the interaction of the head teacher with pupils and staff. Meet the head teacher, as he or she will have an immense influence on the ethos and culture of the school and therefore on the educational experience and pastoral well-being of your child.'

Peter Hamilton, Head teacher of Haberdashers' Aske's Boys' School,

a boys' private secondary school in Elstree

Choosing your school

▶ League tables don't tell you the whole picture. For example they don't tell you:
   ▷ the students' backgrounds
   ▷ the students' IQs
   ▷ the school's background
   ▷ the bigger picture – how this year's results compare with previous years
   ▷ how many students used tutors or had additional input and help
   ▷ what subjects have been taken, given that some subjects such as media studies or PE may be considered 'softer' options.

For league table information, it is best to check out the English and maths scores. You should be looking for more than 50% of children passing A*–C grades in English and maths at GCSE. Make sure you look at the important figures – look at GCSE for A*–C grades, not A*–G.

▶ Check the number of SEN students and EAL students in each school.
▶ Check the level of staff turnover and discipline levels in the Ofsted report.
▶ Visit a school while it is in session: it is a more accurate picture of a typical day.
▶ It is important to visit three or four schools to enable you to compare the options and to consider which one would best suit your child.

10 THINGS TO REMEMBER

1 *Researching the right school for your child can be very time consuming so start investigating the choices early.*

2 *Use all the information available to you – helpful and informative websites are a good place to start.*

3 *There are a number of people who are trained to advise parents on school options, including local authority Choice Advisers and independent organizations such as Parent Partnership.*

4 *When shortlisting schools look at their most recent Ofsted reports.*

5 *Study league table positions for the schools you are interested in, but remember this is only one aspect of a school and very much dependent on their catchment area and intake. It is not necessarily a judgement on their value added and pastoral care.*

6 *Remember when viewing a school's own website and prospectus that they are written by the school and therefore have a bias.*

7 *Where possible always visit a school during the school day – that way you really see it in action, warts and all!*

8 *During visits always look at the way the staff are interacting with the students, the behaviour of the students and whether their learning is stimulating.*

9 *Take the opinions of other parents with caution – you will always find parents with positive and negative experiences of a particular school. What matters is why they are positive or negative and whether these factors would affect your child's happiness in this school.*

10 *Always listen to your head **and** your heart – you will have an instinctive feeling whether a school is right or wrong for your child.*

4

How to fill in the application forms successfully

In this chapter you will learn:
- *about the importance of checking you have up-to-date information*
- *about the differences in form-filling across local authorities*
- *about the importance of ranking schools on your form*
- *how to apply for the different types of schools.*

You've done your homework: read the prospectus; 'Googled' 'til midnight; visited on the open days; compared league table positions; checked admissions criteria and decided which bits of gossip to believe and which to dismiss. It is now time for action – putting your plans into reality and filling in the forms!

Don't be fooled – even form-filling has rules and room for plenty of potential disasters for those not being careful enough.

State school forms

All local authorities in England are required to have co-ordinated arrangements for secondary admissions. These arrangements can vary greatly depending on your local authority – and they can also change from year to year within a local authority. Every child in a primary state school will be given a Local Authority Secondary Transfer Booklet. If your child attends a school in the local authority you live in, known as your maintaining local authority, this booklet will be given to you via your child's school. If your child goes to a primary school which is not in the same local authority that you reside in, then the local authority should send it directly to you. For the majority of local authorities this guidance booklet goes out when your child starts Year 6 (at the beginning of September) and contains information on the whole transition process.

The Secondary Transfer Booklet contains a variety of information about the different types of schools in the local authority, including:

▶ *the process of secondary transfer*
▶ *what to do if you want to apply for schools in a different local authority*
▶ *a timetable of deadlines*
▶ *offers and appeal-making.*

It will also tell you when you will find out which school your child will be offered – usually on 'statutory common offer day' at the beginning of March, and it will give you a list of dates and times of open evenings for all of their secondary schools. Most importantly, this booklet contains the actual form you need to complete – either electronically or manually. This is often called the CAF (Common Application Form). Don't lose it!

You may also have been given a talk by your child's primary head teacher about secondary transition. This usually takes place as the end of Year 5 approaches, or at the beginning of Year 6. My advice is to attend this meeting with a notepad and pen. You may be able to learn specific golden nuggets that are locally relevant and hot off the press.

As discussed in Chapter 3, some local authorities offer Choice Advisers – members of the local authority who hold meetings in primary schools to advise parents about their choices for secondary schools. It is always worth enquiring if your own local authority provides such a service.

Private school forms

For all private schools, you must contact the schools directly in order to receive an application form. Alternatively, you may be able to download a form from their website. At no stage does your local authority get involved. Be aware that some secondary private schools will accept children earlier than age 11, therefore you need to research if they have a 10+ entrance exam. In some cases it is preferable to sit your child for this exam as it may be less stressful than sitting the 11+, where competition is greater.

Along with a completed application form, each private school will ask that you pay a deposit in advance of your child sitting their exam. It is for this reason they are happy for you to complete these forms ahead of time. This clearly separates them from the state sector where the main form is only submitted between allocated dates in September and October. For some state schools, you can send in your application literally years before the date of exams, although submitting early will not put your child's application any higher up in the pecking order – in the end the places will be allocated on ability. Thus, unless stated otherwise by the school, the sensible move may be to send in your application about three months prior to the entrance exam – they never turn good money away and anyone who wishes to sit their exams can!

Things can get slightly messy when dealing with private school consortiums. For most independent schools you apply separately and sit exams at their premises. Some, mainly girls' schools, operate as consortiums. This means that one exam can be taken to cover several schools, but you will still need to pay each school for its consideration and fill in a separate application form.

Warning! Common misconception

Many believe that your child should sit the exam at the school you favour the most in a consortium, as this will influence the school's decision. This is utterly denied by private schools who state that each application is purely judged on academic merit and interview performance.

Completing the state school forms

After receiving your CAF from your local authority, usually in September, you will have a strict deadline to complete it – usually mid October.

On this form you will be asked to list in order of preference the secondary schools that you would like your child to attend. The number of schools you may list varies between local authorities, but the minimum number is usually three and the maximum is usually six, as in the case of London local authorities. You will be asked to either return the form to your child's school if it is in the local authority where you live, or you can return it directly to the local authority. You can also complete and submit it electronically online.

Your maintaining local authority will then manage the co-ordination process. Applications for schools are passed to the admissions authority for each of the schools listed on your form and it is this admissions authority which determines whether a place can be offered. For community schools that is the local authority itself. For other types of schools – like foundation or academy schools – the admissions authority may be the governing body or a charitable committee. These are the bodies that set the admissions criteria for the individual school to decide which children can attend the school.

Where the school is oversubscribed, the school can use their admission criteria to determine the order in which applicants can be offered places. This information is then passed back to your maintaining local authority. The maintaining local authority co-ordinates the offers by holding the highest preference offer on your form and releasing all other lower-preference offers, so that these places can be offered to other applicants.

Warning! More state forms!

Some state schools require you to complete their own application form as well as the local authority CAF. Make sure you check with all of your chosen schools if this is the case. They will not consider your application form if you have not completed theirs as well as the CAF.

How to rank state schools

A word of advice – always put your first choice school as number one, even if you think the chances of getting in are slim. As stated above, the whole system of offering places is organized by your local authority and individual schools do not find out where you have ranked them. They simply judge by your application whether you meet their criteria – be they based on ability, catchment area or sibling policy. They then communicate back to your authority whether your request has been successful.

The local authority will only offer out to you the highest-ranked school on your list, so if you have cautiously put a safer bet higher in your ranking, you won't be offered the long shot even if you were lucky enough to get it, as those above will be offered first. Naming only one school, or naming the same school more than once, will not increase your chance of being offered a place.

Insight

When I was filling out the CAF for my daughter's secondary transfer, parents of older children constantly told me to rank my safe option as number one as the schools would see where I had ranked them. While this was the practice in the past, it is absolutely no longer true.

Warning! Don't get your child to fill in the forms for you

If your child's English is stronger than your own, you may be tempted to ask them to complete the CAF for you. This is not wise as your child will not be aware of the intricate details involved. Should you be unsuccessful with your choices and wish to go to appeal, admitting to filling in the forms incorrectly as you didn't understand them are weak grounds. Instead, speak to a member of the local authority who will advise you on the whole process and assist you with the completion of the forms.

Expert opinion: consider all your options

'As a parent and a head teacher, I know that there is nothing more stressful than securing the right school for your child. It seems as though everyone else is ahead of the game or already in the know. Neither of these things is necessarily true, however, but they do express something of parents' sense of confusion.

The main difficulty of secondary transfer stems from our lack of control of something so important to our children's welfare. We are used to being able to exert choice in the important areas of our lives, but while we are free to choose any school we want, we cannot guarantee a place in our chosen schools. And therein lies the difficulty and our discomfort with the system – we would all like our first choice.

An important message I would like to get across is this: while it is important to pay attention to your first choice, many problems occur if parents have not made sure that they put as much thought and care into identifying alternatives as into their first choice. Parents sometimes put all their eggs in one basket thinking that they can somehow come up with an alternative if their child does not get this first choice. This is not an effective strategy as time is short and places few by the time you know what school you've been allocated. This is where knowing the system and the range of schools on offer really does help. The more you explore, the greater the range of options you will consider.'

Oliver Blond, Head teacher of The Henrietta Barnett School,
a girls' state selective secondary school in North London

Expert opinion: preference order

'Transfer from primary school to secondary school is stressful. Advice comes from many quarters: other parents, family members, primary schools, secondary schools, books. Sometimes this advice is mutually contradictory.

(Contd)

The introduction of the Common Application Form (CAF) has made it easier for boroughs and for schools – and more straightforward in many ways for parents – but I find that, at open evenings and on other occasions, some parents find it difficult to understand how the preference order comes into play. It is not straightforward, indeed it isn't intuitively obvious how it works.

The very helpful notes from my borough, Enfield, include the following:

"Ranking your schools in order of preference is very important because only one offer will be made and this will be from the highest preference school for which your child has qualified under the admission criteria.

All preferences will be considered. If applications for a school exceed the number of available places, the admission criteria will be applied to decide which children are eligible to be offered a place. If your child is eligible for more than one of the schools you have nominated, they will be offered a place at whichever of these schools was ranked higher on your form. All lower ranking preferences are then withdrawn."

Because this is complicated, I find that every year a few parents put another school as their first preference, perhaps because someone at that school told them that they must. Latymer is therefore placed further down their preference list. The child then sits the entrance tests for Latymer, and may do extremely well but then qualifies for the higher preference school so gets an offer there.

I feel very sorry for the child in these circumstances; all that stress of taking tests and, because of the rules applied to the CAF, the child was always going to get an offer at their first preference school.

I have three words of advice to parents:

1 *read the oversubscription criteria for each school in which you are interested*

Differences in form-filling across local authorities in England

1) TIMING

Secondary transfer application forms can vary in deadlines, but in the main are required to be completed in the last two weeks of October. In Wales the closing date is early January.

2) NAMES OF FORMS

Many secondary transfer forms are called the CAF (Common Application Form) but other names are used too: for example, in Bristol it is called the Application Form for Transfer to Secondary Education.

3) NUMBER OF RANKED PREFERENCES

In some local authorities you are allowed up to three school choices to rank in order of preference on your form. In others, for example London, you may list up to six.

4) HOW YOU RECEIVE YOUR OFFERS

Offers will be given out on National Offer Day in England. In some cases an offer will be transmitted electronically using email, in others it will be sent by post to the parents' home address or sent to the primary school.

5) *FILLING IN APPLICATION FORMS*

Some local authorities only allow you to complete application forms online.

6) *SOME LOCAL AUTHORITIES DO NOT TRANSFER AT 11+*

In Bedford, for example, the school system ranges from lower school (Reception to Year 4), to middle school (Year 5 – Year 8) and then to upper school (Year 9 up to sixth form). As there are no secondary schools in Bedfordshire County Council local authority areas, parents who wish their children to attend a secondary school at Year 7 must apply to another local authority.

7) *SOME LOCAL AUTHORITIES HAVE AN ACADEMIC BANDING SYSTEM*

Pupils in these local authorities will take the QCA (Qualifications and Curriculum Authority) tests for mathematics and reading in the summer term of Year 5. Each child will be placed in one of five bands depending on their scores and all secondary schools will divide the number of places available by these five bands and then allocate offers to each band separately, based on their admissions criteria. The rationale behind this is to provide a balanced intake of children of differing abilities. This is currently the case in Greenwich and Lewisham.

8) *SOME LOCAL AUTHORITIES ALLOW CHILDREN TO SIT THE 11+ IN EARLY OCTOBER*

After sitting the 11+ in early October, pupils receive their scores in November via their primary school. These scores will tell parents if their child has met the academic standard necessary for admission into their preferred grammar school, but does not actually offer them a place. Other considerations such as order of preference, the allocation rules for the preferred school and how realistic your preferences are, will affect the final offer which

Hounslow Libraries
Our website:
hounslow.gov.uk/libraries

Self Service Receipt for Check Out

Name: **********2721

Title: The 5am club : own your
morning, elevate your life

Item: C0000002868452

Due Back: 11/12/2021

Title: Get your child into the school
you want

Item: C0000002524806

Due Back: 11/12/2021

Total Check Out: 2
20/11/2021 13:34:59

Thank you for using Hounslow Libraries
self service kiosks.

will be given in March. A local authority that uses this type of procedure is Buckinghamshire. Those children who do not pass the 11+ will be offered a place at an upper school instead of a grammar school.

Interesting statistics in England for National Offer Day (3 March 2008)

▶ *82% of families received an offer of a place at their highest preference school*
▶ *94% of families received an offer of a place at one of their top three preference schools*
▶ *95.6% of families received an offer of a place at one of their preferred schools (NB different local authorities offer different numbers of preferences).*

Figures published by the Department for Children, Schools and Families (May 2008).

The Scottish secondary transfer timetable

In Scotland, children transfer from primary school to secondary school at Primary 7 stage, between the ages of 11½ and 12½. Transition takes place in August and parents with children transferring from Primary 7 to secondary schools will receive information on transfer arrangements in the December prior to their child's entry to secondary school. Forms normally need to be completed by March. Primary schools will tell you the name of the secondary school to which your child would normally transfer. You have the right to make a placing request to attend any secondary school, but there is no guarantee of success.

The Welsh secondary transfer timetable

The National Assembly for Wales takes responsibility for all school admissions in Wales. Here children transfer from primary school to secondary school at the same time as in England. However, there are certain timetable changes. In Wales forms need to be submitted by mid January and offers are not sent out until the middle of March.

Case study: state school admissions in Sheffield

In Sheffield, admission for all state schools is run through the Secondary Admissions department of Sheffield City Council. It requires parents to complete a CAF listing up to three schools that they would prefer their child to go to, ranking them in order of preference. If parents choose to apply for a voluntary aided school, they must attach additional information and forms. Parents have the right to apply for a place at any school, not just their catchment school (which is where they will have priority). However, places are not reserved in catchment schools for parents who apply to other schools and are unsuccessful. Forms need to be completed by mid October and offers are sent out in the post on National Offer Day at the beginning of March.

Where a school is oversubscribed, the school will use its admission criteria to determine the order in which applicants can be offered places. Where no offer can be made for any of the three preferences stated on the CAF, a place will be allocated at a catchment school only if there are still places available or at the nearest community school in Sheffield that has available spaces.

Case study: state school admissions in London

In London, admission for all state schools is run centrally by an arrangement called the Pan London Admissions System. It requires parents to list up to six schools that they would prefer their child to go to on one form, ranking them in order of preference. The application form is obtained from and sent back to the local authority, which manages the co-ordination process. Forms have a strict deadline – usually mid October. Applications for schools within the local authority are passed to the admission authority for each of the schools – for community schools, that is the local authority itself. Applications for schools in other boroughs are sent to the local authority that maintains those schools ('the maintaining LA') via a computerized system called the Pan London Register.

The admission authority for each of the schools listed determines whether a place can be offered. Where the school is oversubscribed, the school uses its admission criteria to determine the order in which applicants can be offered places. These admissions criteria differ from school to school. They can also differ between local authorities: for example, Greenwich and Lewisham are the only London authorities to use the banding system. This information is then passed back to the maintaining LA. The maintaining LA co-ordinates the offers by holding the highest preference offer on the pupil's form and releasing all other lower-preference offers, so that these places can be offered to other applicants.

Supporting documents

In order to meet the admissions criteria for some schools, an additional supporting document may be required. This may be:

▶ *from your school – asking about your child's academic position in class, their additional responsibilities held in school as well as clubs and groups they have attended*
▶ *from a religious community leader – supporting any religious applications*
▶ *from a sports coach or club leader – supporting any extra-curricular claims on your application.*

It is very important to find out if any of the schools on your list require a supporting document. If a report is required from school, it is wise to flag up to the head teacher or class teacher writing the report the full range of your child's talents – be it music, sports, drama, languages and so on. Often these teachers don't know about your child's pre- and post-school activities and these need to be highlighted in applications.

Insight

You may be asked to prove regular attendance at a particular place of worship. This cannot be achieved last minute so it is really important to find out well ahead of time what the requirements are.

Parent case study

'I wanted my son to go a local state selective school. The entrance criteria are solely based on academic ability and are judged by sitting an exam. I was worried that he might not be successful in the exam, although I knew he was a hard worker and had practised with both verbal and non-verbal exercises. My second choice school was a local community secondary school where the criteria set by the local authority were special needs and looked-after children, siblings and then catchment area. In previous years my postcode came well within the accepted boundary for the school and it appeared likely my son would be offered a place. I was worried that if I ranked the state selective school as number one, then our second choice would not offer us a place. Therefore I put our local community school as first choice, and the state selective as second.

At the beginning of March my son was offered a place at his first choice. I assumed that he had simply been unsuccessful in the entrance examination to the local state selective school, but out of curiosity I wanted to find out how close he had come to an offer – perhaps he could be put on the waiting list. When I rang the admissions officer she told me that my son had been successful in the exam and they had offered him a place. They could only conclude that our local authority had offered us an alternative school which we had ranked higher on our list. I was devastated and wished I had known this before I ranked my schools in order of preference. Sadly it was too late to make any changes.'

Fiona, mother of James (Year 6)

How to apply for a music or dance award or place

Many private schools offer places to children showing talent in music or dance. Music scholarships will usually be offered to children following an audition, but these children will also need to qualify through the academic entrance examination first. The value of a scholarship will vary greatly from school to school.

For state schools it is very different. These places for music or dance aptitude are offered solely on aptitude for music and/or dance and are not related to academic ability. The ranking of the candidate's musical aptitude – in an objective test administered by the school – will ultimately lead to the offer of a place to candidates who have specifically requested to be considered for a priority place under this musical category.

In the case of state selective schools, places will be offered to pupils who show exceptional musical talent and achievement provided that, on the evidence shown by achievement in the entrance tests, they are also capable of maintaining the academic progress expected of the rest of the school's intake. The number of places available will vary from school to school and year to year. It is important to check with the schools each year to find out the latest situation, but places are usually oversubscribed, often by as much as ten children for every one place.

HOW TO APPLY FOR A MUSICAL SCHOLARSHIP PLACE

Most state schools require you to complete an additional application form or questionnaire to the general CAF. Private schools will ask you to fill in a music scholarship form in addition to their registration form.

WHAT ARE THE SCHOOLS LOOKING FOR AND WHAT WILL THE AUDITION ENTAIL?

Schools offer musical awards in the hope that the recipient will take a full and active part in the school's musical activities during their time at the school. The actual audition will vary from school to school, but may include a set piece on a pupil's main instrument, together with an own-choice piece.

Sometimes candidates may be given a written musical aptitude test which will involve the discrimination of changes to rhythms and pitches and an awareness of the number of notes in chords. Questions can relate to pitch, rhythm, texture and melody. More commonly, pupils will be given an aural test rather than a written one. Usually, a knowledge of music theory is not required for these tests.

Many private schools state that as a guideline a pupil should have achieved at least Grade 5 distinction level, but this will depend on the instrument as well as previous opportunity and experience. For state schools this is not always the case, with some places being offered to pupils who have reached Grade 3 level or below; they may well be looking for a child's future potential and an eclectic musical mix for their coming year.

For dance auditions, pupils are usually asked to prepare and deliver a short dance and then may be asked to learn a new one for the examiners to evaluate.

Pupil case study: dance audition

'I was one of 12 children in my dance audition. We were all given a couple of minutes to warm up and to stretch our legs. Then we were shown to some chairs and called in one by one to deliver our two-minute prepared dance. I performed a contemporary dance to the music of *High School Musical*. I brought the CD with me as they needed the music in advance. Once everyone had performed their individual dance we were called back into the main hall together and taught a new dance. We practised this new dance around five times and then we were given two minutes to improvise our own ending to it. We were then asked to leave the room and come back again individually to perform this newly-learnt dance with our own individual ending. The whole audition took about half an hour.'

Freya (Year 7)

Pupil case study: music audition

'When I did my music audition for Mill Hill County I felt really nervous. I sat in the large hall with six scared faces surrounding me. Then I walked into the practice room and there were instruments and a keyboard set up to practise on. Next a sixth-form student opened the door and called my name. I was really nervous and I almost cried. My hands were shaking and I couldn't keep still. There was another boy with me and we were told to sit down on the chairs. We had about one minute to relax before I was called in for the aural section of the audition.

There were two rooms for aural auditions. I was sent to one, and the boy was sent to the other audition room. A woman came up to me and sent me into the audition room. Then she placed a chair in the middle of the room. She told me to sit down and she then took her place at the stool behind the wooden piano. First she played three songs and I had to clap them all back. Then she played three final songs and I had to sing them back. Finally, she played three more songs and I had to tell her about the dynamics. When I had finished I went back to the practice room to collect the music for the song I was playing. Another sixth-form student came up to me and led me to the chairs in the large corridor. There were children there my age and suddenly I didn't feel quite so alone, as they were all nervous just like me. There was a hall at the end of the corridor. I was called in and there were three examiners in the room. I gave the examiners copies of the piece I was playing. I then sat at the grand piano and started to play. I was only allowed to play one piece, any choice as long as it was less than two minutes. When I finished a wave of relief hit me. It had ended finally.'

Bridey (Year 6)

Frequently asked questions

Can I apply for both state and private schools?

Yes. The systems are completely separate. For state schools you complete a CAF. For private schools you contact them directly. It is a good safety option to secure a place at a state school as backup in case your child is not successful in their entrance exams for private schools.

Will the state schools know where I have ranked them?

No. Only your maintaining local authority knows this information. All the schools will receive is your application and they will base their decision on whether you meet their entrance criteria. Therefore you will not be penalized by other schools for not putting their school at the top.

What is a maintaining local authority?

It is the authority that you live in and it is this authority that handles the whole process of secondary transfer in the state system.

When should I apply?

It depends, as each local authority differs – so check first, but it is usually around the middle to end of October.

How will I know if the Local Authority Admissions Team has received my form?

Applications made online will usually be acknowledged by return email. This is a quick and safe method of knowing that your application has been received. Proof of posting cannot be considered as proof of receipt unless accompanied by official proof of delivery. If you send a stamped self-addressed postcard with your completed form, this will be returned to you by some local authorities as confirmation of receipt of your application.

Do I have to express more than one preference?

You do not have to express a preference for more than one school. However, it is strongly advisable that you name more than one because if you do not meet the criteria of your preferred school your local authority will then offer you a school that is the most local to your address which has places available. This may be far from acceptable to you so giving the local authority other options is seen as sensible.

How many places are available at each school?

The admissions number for each school varies and you must speak to each school individually.

If I submit my form before the deadline do I have a better chance of success?

No. No applications will be considered until the date of the deadline and all will be treated as first round allocations.

What happens if my application is received after the closing date?

Your application may be disadvantaged and you may not be offered a place at your preferred school, even if you meet the entrance criteria.

Can I change my preference?

Each local authority is different. Some say a change of preference must be made in writing, some say you need to do it online. It is important to make amendments before the closing date, otherwise it will be treated as a late application and may not be considered in the first round of allocations.

What can I do if my child is not offered a place at my preferred school?

You will be offered a place at an alternative school by your maintaining local authority. Your then have choices – accept the alternative place, ask about availability of places at alternative schools, have your child's name held on a waiting list for a place at your preferred school or appeal to an independent appeal panel against the decision to refuse a place.

What if I move to a new home when my child is in Year 6 but I miss the October deadline?

You can still move your child from one school to another outside the usual times. However, you'll need to talk to the relevant local authority first.

How will I find out about secondary transition in the state sector if my child is currently attending a private primary school?

If your child goes to a private primary school, your local authority will make contact with you through your school via a letter usually around the end of Year 5. This letter will explain the process of secondary school transition and will urge you to make contact if you would like to receive a Common Application Form.

Form-filling

▶ *Find out how many forms you need to fill in for each school.*

▶ *Find out the application deadline and stick to it.*

▶ *Find out the different methods of form-filling – online or in writing.*

▶ *Remember to use the CAF for the maintaining local authority you live in, not based on the local authority of your child's school.*

▶ *Double-check the admissions criteria for the schools you are listing on your form – they can change from year to year and it could be a wasted preference if you do not meet a school's criteria.*

▶ *Remember, you can check all the information by looking at your local authority website.*

▶ *Be honest when ranking your schools – the borough will always offer you the school ranked highest on your list.*

▶ *If sitting your child for private consortiums, make sure you apply to each school required in the consortium separately, even though there is just the one exam.*

▶ *Make sure you know when to fill in forms – each local authority can be different. For example, in 2008: in Bristol and London forms needed to be completed by 24 October; in Doncaster 17 October; in Wales by December.*

▶ *If you rent a house in the catchment area in order to meet a school's admissions criteria, make sure you know how long you must reside in the area in order to secure your child's place, now and in the future.*

10 THINGS TO REMEMBER

1 *The process of applying for private schools and state schools is completely different.*

2 *To apply to sit an exam for a private school, the school will need to be contacted directly and usually a financial deposit will be requested.*

3 *To apply for state schools, including state selective schools, a Common Application Form (CAF) needs to be completed. This is given to a child in the September of Year 6.*

4 *Sometimes, in addition to the CAF, state schools require their own application forms to be completed. It is important to check this out.*

5 *If applying for a faith school supporting paperwork is often required.*

6 *There is a strict deadline for when the CAF needs to be completed – this is usually the middle of October when your child is in Year 6.*

7 *When ranking school preference, remember the schools do not know where you have ranked them.*

8 *Your local authority will only offer you one school. This will only be a school from your preference list if you meet the admissions criteria for that school.*

9 *If you do not meet the admissions criteria for your preferred school, your local authority will offer you another school within the authority which is not oversubscribed.*

10 *Private school offers are usually sent out at the end of February. State offers are circulated on National Offer Day which is in the first week of March.*

5

How to help your child pass the examinations

In this chapter you will learn:
- *the similarities and differences in exam style for different types of schools and how best to prepare your child*
- *what's in the tests: verbal, non-verbal, maths and English*
- *how to understand your child's scores*
- *why, when and how to get tutors.*

We all have memories of sitting exams. Some of us went through these same exams when we were 11, others will remember public exams at the ages of 16 and 18, for example: O levels and CSEs (for us oldies), GCSEs and A levels. Each child will view exams in a different way and with varying degrees of fear. Our job is to prepare them as much as possible for the exams – both in terms of content and procedure. We must also stress that whatever the outcome, we will still love them and be proud of them.

The similarities and differences in exam style for different types of schools

For many state selective schools, the exam fun and games start from October half-term with verbal and non-verbal tests. These tests are usually open to anyone who wants to sit the exams – and are an opportunity to weed out the weaker candidates, leaving the top ones to fight it out in the second round of exams, which are usually English and maths based.

The verbal and non-verbal tests give prospective schools an idea of the child's potential and intelligence, whereas the maths and English tests are largely an extension of what is taught at key stage 2 in primary schools. These papers establish how well the child has absorbed the education that they received at primary school.

Did you know?

The wiggles and squiggles of non-verbal reasoning tests are actually an indication of your child's potential – a measure of their intelligence. The verbal reasoning test is a measure of how well they will learn new information and is seen as an indication of the likely ease with which children will be able to acquire new concepts and understand new ideas across a range of school subjects.

Private schools' exams tend to be in January and they are usually either their own exams or the Common Entrance Exam. These tend to be maths and English tests, although a science test may also be included on occasion. Unlike the state selective schools where interviews are now banned, a candidate will often be asked back for an interview before a decision is made whether to offer a place.

Insight

When researching schools for my daughter, I found that private schools are less likely to test verbal reasoning and non-verbal reasoning aptitudes. When they do, they incorporate them into their other tests rather than testing them on their own.

How best to prepare your child for these different types of tests

One word – PRACTISE! It is essential that your child is familiar with these types of tests. Verbal and non-verbal reasoning tests are not on the National Curriculum syllabus and are rarely taught in schools. Therefore those without experience are disadvantaged. It is essential that your child is given an opportunity to familiarize themselves with these types of questions.

To do this, you can buy past examination papers directly from secondary schools or purchase practice test papers in leading bookstores. You will need to start this preparation long before the exams. While the amount of time to prepare for these exams will differ from child to child, it is not an exaggeration to suggest that you may start preparing your child up to two years before the actual exams.

It is also important to make sure you know well ahead of time what the tests will be at your preferred schools: some do verbal and non-verbal, some just verbal, and some only maths and English. Make sure you check it out – especially as individual schools can change what they test from year to year. You also will need to check the dates of the tests. For state selective schools these can differ greatly between local authorities, and private schools also sit at different times. Liaise directly with your local authority or private school for up-to-date information.

Which types of practice papers to buy

They're bright, they're colourful and they're in the majority of bookshops. But which practice papers are the best and which should you buy?

Practice papers and study books fall into two categories:

▶ *preparation for the 11+ or secondary school exams*
▶ *preparation for the end-of-key stage 2 SATs tests.*

While the first is clearly written for entrance exam preparation, don't dismiss the second type of books as they can also be useful, providing maths and English support and past SATs papers which will also be relevant to secondary school exams.

RECOMMENDED SCHOOL ENTRANCE EXAM PRACTICE PAPERS

▶ *Bond materials (see page 201 for a selection)*
▶ *Athey Educational practice papers*
▶ *GL Assessment (previously NFER-NELSON)*

- *Learning together 11+ and 12+ preparation tests*
- *CGP*
- *Rising Stars UK Ltd publications*
- *Individual school's past papers (where available)*
- *Common Entrance Exam papers*
- *MW Education Papers.*

RECOMMENDED END-OF-KEY STAGE 2 SATS PRACTICE PAPERS

- *Schofield and Sims*
- *W H Smith*
- *Bond*
- *CPG.*

Many of these materials come in different types and formats – they may be parent help books, assessment papers, test papers, timed tests or problem-solving activities. Whatever the style, their purpose is to introduce your child to the types of questions they will encounter at the 11+ exams and SATs, and give them an opportunity to practise these types of questions. Some books go one step further and give a full description of the sorts of questions that come up and also give hints to parents and children on how best to answer them.

It is also important to note that many private schools produce their own papers and example copies of these papers can be found on the school's website.

Expert opinion: advice from GL Assessment

'There are a number of things parents can do to support their children in the run up to a test. For a start, it helps to familiarize children with the style and the format of the 11+, making the real test seem less intimidating on the day. Tackling a practice paper under timed conditions gives children valuable experience of managing their time effectively and it can help them to develop an approach to the test that ensures they have enough time to answer every question.

Practice test scores will also create a picture of your child's strengths and weaknesses, giving you a clear understanding of how you can help them. And it almost goes without saying that achieving good scores in practice tests can boost a child's confidence and reduce their anxiety in the run-up to the test day.

It's also important to talk to your children about their feelings about being tested and offer support and encouragement – they need to know that doing their best is what counts the most. It is also a good idea to plan something fun for after the test, to give them something to look forward to.'

Amanda Power, GL Assessment

Encourage your child to mark their own work

All practice papers and booklets come with answers. For many parents that's a godsend as we often struggle with the answers! A useful tip is to allow your child to mark their own work. That way they are able to identify their errors and then go on to correct them. As long as they understand their mistakes, they can move on to the next test. If your child is unable to understand their error, then you need to go over it with them – otherwise they will repeat the error and not learn from their mistakes.

Insight

I found it useful to ask my daughter to complete the grids at the back of her Bond test papers, as they are a wonderful way of visually showing progress and allowed my daughter to see how she was improving.

COMPLETING THE PRACTICE PAPERS: HOW MUCH SHOULD YOU NAG?

Your nagging schedule should depend on the needs of your child, but as a general rule little and often usually works best, particularly in the early days. Encourage your child to work on practice papers at regular intervals during the week and for no more than perhaps half an hour at a time. Establish a weekly routine and stick to it. As the exams draw nearer, you may need to adjust your weekly routine, perhaps moving to a daily and 'as long as it takes' routine, rather than little and often.

What's in the tests: verbal, non-verbal, maths and English

Most tests are usually around 45 minutes and very rarely go on longer than an hour.

VERBAL REASONING TESTS

Verbal reasoning could be commonly known as 'solving word puzzles'. The paper tests the child's ability to select the right word from multiple choices of similar ones, find chains of words, perform word association, choose synonyms and antonyms, complete sentences and generally show a depth of understanding of the English language. The best preparation for this element of the entrance examination is an extensive vocabulary developed from reading a wide range of books.

In terms of structure, verbal reasoning questions fall into two types: either multiple choice where a choice of answers is given and the pupil needs to identify the correct one, or a standard layout/format where no answers are given and the pupil must fill in their own answers.

Verbal reasoning is often broken into four groups: sorting words, selecting words, anagrams and coded sequences.

NON-VERBAL REASONING TESTS

Non-verbal reasoning tests the child's ability to solve IQ test-type problems, which consist of patterns, pictures, shapes and symbols. The questions relate to identifying families of shapes, completing sequences, choosing the odd one out or developing rules which connect pairs of objects and then applying that rule to subsequent pairs. Most non-verbal reasoning questions will be multiple choice. Non-verbal reasoning questions are often broken into the following groups: similarities, analogies, sequences, hidden shapes, matrices, reflected shapes, nets of cubes, codes and combined shapes.

Insight

You will find with non-verbal tests that the question type which usually confuses children the most is the nets of cubes. This is very common and the best way to help your child is to clearly write on the nets which sides will attach to each other, thus through elimination deciding which nets are possible and which are not.

MATHS TESTS

The maths that is tested in entrance examinations is similar in content to the maths taught at school in the numeracy curriculum. Children are tested on their knowledge of: multiplication, division, addition and subtraction, decimals, fractions, ratios, converting units, charts and data handling, shape and space and measurement. Occasionally some key stage 3 maths will be included, usually algebra questions.

For the maths test special equipment may be required – this can include a ruler, set square, protractor, pair of compasses and calculator. Check with each school as equipment requirements can vary.

Maths test preparation – the essentials

▶ *Know your tables inside out.*
▶ *Identify your child's strengths and weaknesses – the topic is vast and your child may be excellent with shape, angle and data handling questions but unable to do long multiplication. Identify weaknesses and then blitz!*

ENGLISH TESTS

As with maths, the literacy skills that are tested in secondary school entrance exams are covered in schools as part of the literacy framework. These are usually divided up into a comprehension and a story.

Comprehension

This is an exercise or test that usually consists of: a passage or passages of text, part of a story, a poem, a piece of information or explanation or a description. Pupils are asked to read the text independently and demonstrate their understanding by answering questions. Question types may vary, but are likely to include 'retrieval' questions, whereby children will be asked to find the relevant answer that is clearly given in the text. They will also be asked to use higher order thinking skills by answering questions that require 'inference' and 'deduction'. Children will also be asked to write their own opinions – their opinion itself is not being judged, rather how well they can explain their opinion using evidence from the original text.

Insight

I found that encouraging my child to consider herself as a mini Sherlock Holmes helped her with comprehension answers. I told her that even though the answers weren't staring her in the face, there were clues in the passages which needed to be picked up and would lead to the right answers. To start the process always look at the key words in the questions and then find them in the text.

Writing

This is the second part of the English test where pupils are asked to compose a piece of writing. This will test the pupil's ability with spelling, punctuation, grammar, vocabulary and handwriting. The number of titles offered in exams varies: some allow candidates to choose from many different titles, sometimes there is no choice at all. Written tasks may be fiction or non-fiction and the genre may vary, for example: a diary entry, a letter, a playscript, a report and so on. Often children will be asked to continue the story they read for the comprehension. Time for writing also varies in exams: it could be between 20 minutes and an hour. It is important to keep an eye on time.

English test preparation – the essentials

Your child does not need to be an expert at English. They simply need to learn the rules for good writing and good comprehension answers.

In comprehension work children need to:

▶ *refer to the text for answers*
▶ *write their answer using their own words, not copying from the text*
▶ *give opinions which they can support with examples from the text.*

In writing work children need to:

▶ *use paragraphs*
▶ *use a range of National Curriculum Level 5 punctuation – this includes full stops, commas, ellipses, question marks,*

(Contd)

exclamation marks, speech marks, dashes, brackets, semicolons and colons
- ► know the genre and stick to its structure
- ► know the audience and write appropriately – for example, is it formal or informal?
- ► plan their writing – getting started is always the hardest part; it is important to write a mini-plan
- ► use joined-up handwriting
- ► include similes, metaphors and alliteration where appropriate
- ► start sentences with impressive openers such as '-ing' words or '-ly' words, for example 'suddenly', 'awkwardly', or 'deciding to'
- ► check their writing – children hate editing their work, but it is essential.

Dealing with exam day nerves

- ► Do your homework. Speak to someone who has an older child who has been through the exam previously – give your child a full idea of what to expect.
- ► Make sure your child has a good night's sleep the day before the exam.
- ► Wake your child early on the day of the exam, allowing plenty of time.
- ► Give your child a good breakfast.
- ► Arrive at the exam with plenty of time to spare, so both you and your child will feel relaxed. Be careful not to arrive at the exam too early as seeing and talking to other anxious people will only raise anxiety levels.
- ► Make sure your child has the correct equipment with them.
- ► Remind your child to read the questions carefully and leave plenty of time to check their answers.
- ► Remind your child to be aware of time – not to spend too much time on one particular section of the test.

- ► *Encourage your child to keep going – even if they find some areas of the test hard, other parts that come later may be easier.*
- ► *Ensure your child is comfortable during the exam. Have they been to the toilet? Encourage them to check that they are not too hot or too cold. Allow them to layer dress so they can take off items where necessary.*
- ► *Encourage your child to plan their story. A couple of minutes spent on a plan and rough notes will help their thoughts to flow.*
- ► *Remind them you are proud of them – whatever the outcome!*

Expert opinion: the admissions process at a private girls' secondary school

'Parents may find it hard to believe that for many, the whole transfer procedure is THE most stressful time in a head teacher's year! We too want what is best for your children, and making sure we have the right children in our schools is the most important thing that we do.

Let me share with you how the process works at my school, a selective, independent single-sex school. Girls sit an entrance exam in English and maths. Sample papers are available on the website, and there is nothing startling about them: a comprehension, a story and various mathematical exercises to grapple with. I am presented with a score out of 100 for both... For me, as head teacher of an academic school, it is usually quite clear from these tests that most applicants have been well-taught. It is also clear which candidates have been tutored and which have not. I look for potential rather than performance, and my staff are experts at spotting examples of "prepared showing off"! We purposely set questions where natural flair can shine through.

The good news is that the examination is only one part of the story. Perhaps the most important elements in our selection procedures are the junior school reports and the interviews. The head teacher

(Contd)

of your child's junior school is asked to provide a full report of their educational story so far. Some heads are better than others at highlighting your child's potential. I like to see the results of any tests, IQ, SATs, reading, other achievements, any relevant hurdles they have overcome, any learning needs, any circumstances that might have affected their progress. I will often pick up the phone and speak to a junior school head. I trust them. They know your child and are very astute at knowing where he or she will make the best progress: academically, socially and emotionally.

We interview applicants whom we believe would thrive, contribute and be happy at Channing. Again, my interview team are very good at spotting potential. Some families worry unduly at being tutored or "prepped" for interview. For us, it is the thirst for knowledge, the enthusiasm and the willingness and capacity to listen and learn that make the difference. That comes naturally to 10- and 11-year-olds (or not!). I have occasionally not offered a place to very able pupils whose attitude and approach to life simply would not fit with our ethos – which values care and consideration for others above all else.'

Barbara Elliott, Head teacher of Channing School,
a private girls' secondary school in North London

How to identify your child's ability

It is very important to have realistic expectations; for that you need to know what level your child is working at. To do this you can:

▶ *Ask the school. Liaise closely with your child's class teacher and head teacher: what do they predict for your child in maths, English and science for the end-of-key stage SATs? Find out your child's reading and spelling age, as well as their current National Curriculum levels in maths, writing and reading. Most schools will have this information, but they often do not volunteer it.*
▶ *Find out for yourself. Set some timed practice tests that can be bought in leading bookstores.*
▶ *Ask a tutor. Most tutors will assess your child and give you useful feedback about their level of attainment.*

How to understand your child's scores: cutting through the jargon of National Curriculum, standardized and percentile scores

Once you know your child's scores, be it a National Curriculum level in writing of 1c, or Level 4a in maths or a standardized score of 114 in spelling, the next step is to find out what they mean! Are these scores good, or bad? What do these scores mean compared to others in their class and indeed across the country? You need to know if they have a realistic chance of passing these secondary school exams. If not, don't make your child sit them – it's not fair! The most common test scores are as follows.

NATIONAL CURRICULUM LEVELS

School assessment is ongoing. At both ends of the academic year, your child will be given a National Curriculum level and based on these scores, your child's school will assess if they have made adequate progress. You may be told what this level is, but what does it really mean?

An average child is expected to make two-thirds of a National Curriculum level progress from year to year. Each level is subdivided into three sections: a, b or c – with 'a' being the highest and 'c' the lowest. By the end of key stage 1 an average child will be scoring 2b, and by the end of key stage 2 in Year 6, an average child will be scoring 4b. The table below explains how well a child is achieving in each year group compared to the national average.

Year 3	
National Curriculum level	Comparison with national expectation
Level 1 or below	Below national expectation
2c/2b	Working towards national expectation
2a/3c	In line with national expectation
3b/3a/4c	Above national expectation
A good Level 4b and above	Significantly above national expectation

Year 4	
National Curriculum level	Comparison with national expectation
Level 2c or below	Below national expectation
2b/2a	Working towards national expectation
3c/3b	In line with national expectation
3a/4c/4b	Above national expectation
4a and above	Significantly above national expectation

Year 5	
National Curriculum level	Comparison with national expectation
Level 2 or below	Below national expectation
3c/3b	Working towards national expectation
3a/4c	In line with national expectation
4b/4a/5c	Above national expectation
A good Level 5b and above	Significantly above national expectation

Year 6	
National Curriculum level	Comparison with national expectation
Below Level 3	Below national expectation
Level 3	Working towards national expectation
Level 4	In line with national expectation
5c/5b	Above national expectation
5a/Level 6	Significantly above national expectation

Insight

I find it easier to simply think in terms of: is my child where they should be for their age? If not, are they ahead of others or are they behind? Knowing where they are in the class can be a red herring as classes vary greatly in ability levels, and just because your child is top of one class don't assume they will be top of a different class.

STANDARDIZED SCORES

In other types of tests and assessments, your child may be given a standardized score. This is often the case for reading and spelling. A standardized score enables you to compare your own child with a large, nationally representative sample of those who have taken the test prior to your child.

A standardized score is calculated by using the child's raw score from the test and combining it using a special formula with their age at the time of testing. This means that their standardized score is compared with other pupils of the same age. A national average score for any standardized test is 100. The ranges of scores from most tests are 70–141. If a child scores between 85 and 115, they are considered in the normal range. If your child is scoring anything above 100, then they are above average. For many entrance exam tests, schools will be looking for scores anywhere above 115. For the top grammar and private schools, scores of 130+ are usually expected.

Check it out!

Some schools will take your child's chronological age into consideration by using standardized scores for their tests, rather than simply using raw scores – the actual number of correctly answered questions. This will benefit children who are younger for the year, typically those who are summer babies. It is therefore useful to check with each school how they score their results.

PERCENTILE RANKS

Some tests are scored as a percentile rank. A percentile rank is the percentage of pupils in the sample who gained a score at the same level or below that of your child's score. Therefore, if your child's performance is at the 75th percentile, for example, then they will have performed as well as, or better than 75% of the sample, having taken age into account. It also means that they are in the top 25% of the country; in other words only 25 children out of 100 would perform better than them.

Parent case study

'All through primary school, I had been told that my child was clever. He sailed through all his homework and he rarely asked me or his father to explain school things to him. End-of-year tests would come and go and at parents' evenings and school reports I was told he was performing above the national average. When it came to choosing secondary schools I decided to sit him for the local state selective schools, based on the positive feedback I had been given so far. My son was unsuccessful in all these exams and it was a bitter blow. With hindsight I should have been more prepared: I should have asked more questions by the time he was in upper primary; I should have asked his teachers for his results and whether he was reaching his full potential. It turns out that my child is in the top 7–10 % of the country, with a standardized score ranging from 119 to 122 for most of his subjects. However, in real terms this was not good enough for the state selective schools I had chosen and it would have saved us all a lot of heartache if I had known this ahead of time.'

Katherine, mother of Jesse (Year 7)

Why, when and how to get tutors

WHY TUTOR?

Secondary school entrance exam preparation is not usually taught at school. It is up to the individual school to decide if they are going to give time to practising these skills with their pupils, and the majority do not. Therefore, it is important for your child to get experience of these types of questions before they sit the exam; learning and practising many different question types will greatly reduce the potential for children to be faced with unexpected question styles during a test.

'I was encouraged by friends who have older children to think ahead of time. By Year 4 my daughter Sophie had a tutor who was beginning to prepare her for the whole 11+ process. Whilst I don't condone the need for a tutor, it did seem to be a given requirement amongst other parents and it certainly made me feel more relaxed. This is because I felt that it was no longer solely my responsibility to help Sophie pass the exams – I now had a paid partner to share my anxieties and angst with.'

Juliette, mother of Sophie (Year 8)

The obvious advantage of one-to-one tutoring is that your child will be taught individually. This means that they will not be lost in a class with other, more demanding children who can take up the teacher's time. In addition, their needs will be met on an individual basis, with their strengths and weaknesses identified and supported. While many schools are spending a great deal of time and resources extending gifted and talented pupils, there is still a chance that these children can be overlooked – and these 'overlooked' children are often the ones who will be sitting exams!

Many parents believe that they don't need a tutor as they can prepare their children for the demands of the examinations themselves. This is possibly true, but don't underestimate the professional tutor/pupil relationship – it is totally different and often more productive than family-led teaching and also less stressful for the parents.

The disadvantage of tutors can be their cost – tutoring is not cheap. The cost of tutoring varies from tutor to tutor, area to area. It is not uncommon for experienced tutors in parts of London to charge up to £50 an hour for one-to-one tutoring. You also need to consider the timeframe for tutoring – it often can go on for up to two years and on a weekly basis – that's a lot of money!

Another thing to think about is why you are tutoring; don't over-tutor your child to get them into a school which won't be right for them. It is important that children develop and progress at their own pace and forcing them to progress faster than they are ready for, will ultimately lead to frustration and unhappiness if they are accepted into a highly competitive, top achieving school and are unable to cope.

Expert opinion: tutoring

'Tutoring for tests for admission to secondary school may result in a place at a selective school when without tutoring the place may not have been gained. Tutoring seems attractive, therefore, and there is no doubt that many parents do use a tutor for their child. But my advice is not to get a tutor.

As children move through the education system they are expected to become more and more self-disciplined, self-reliant and self-motivated. Education is lifelong, or should be. Universities in particular expect students to have all these qualities. I believe that getting a tutor for a child at age ten is not encouraging this process, rather it leads the child to feel that their parents will pay for extra support, with the best intentions, in the hope that it is in the child's best interests. But I believe it can be counter-productive in the long term, both in terms of academic attainment and in terms of mental health.

If a student gains a place at a selective school as a result of coaching which may have inflated their IQ score, they will be in a class with children of higher academic ability than themselves. This has the possible positive effect of encouraging them and enabling them to improve their performance, in line with others in the class. However, there are two possible serious negative effects: they may hope and expect a tutor to be provided by their parents for a subject as soon as they get a grade B for a piece of work; and more seriously, they can't cope as well with the academic work as they should, leading to all sorts of problems with their schooling. The most serious possible drawback is that they could gain a view of themselves which is negative rather than positive in terms of self-esteem. This can be devastating in terms of mental health over a period of years.'

Mark Garbett, Head teacher of The Latymer School,
a state selective secondary school in North London

'Guilt is something many parents feel: guilt at both Mum and Dad working, guilt if things go wrong for your child, guilt if it is perceived that someone else is doing more for their child than you are for yours. Add to this the perceived pecking order of schools in any local region, and unfortunately there are always those people who will brag that their child is at, or going to, the 'best' school. For some parents, the air-conditioning to this heated atmosphere is the private but unregulated tutor – the person who can sort out their child's maths or English, the person who is so experienced at getting children in to St Cake's or St Custard's. It's tempting to buy the helping hand, but it's also likely to bring a shudder to the face of the child's prospective head. Why? Firstly, if a child has to be tutored to get in to a school, how will they survive if their ability has been artificially enhanced and all they do is end up struggling to keep up? Entrance exams are actually the parents' friend. They tell you what the standard is of the school you're applying to, and if your child will be in the right school for them. Tutoring can be as silly as someone going to the doctor but reporting false symptoms. Secondly, it can also be damaging to children. Tested and measured beyond any level previously imposed on UK children, forced to concentrate on the three Rs to the exclusion of much else, our children no longer have time to gather flowers by the wayside. Add to this one or two evening or weekend sessions with a tutor and you risk alienating the child, force-feeding them knowledge they should come to in their own time. One potentially very negative side effect is to teach the child that if at first they don't understand something, then someone else will be brought in to make it easy. Effective learning does not work like that. Children need to learn to persevere and stick at something, developing tenacity and responsibility alongside insight. The result can be confusion rather than greater clarity of understanding. The best way to know if you've chosen the right school for your child? Well, if you think it needs a tutor to get him or her there, it's probably not the right school.'

Jenny Stephen, Headmistress of South Hampstead High School,

a private girls' school in London

WHEN TO TUTOR

The amount of time you need to prepare your child for the exams varies, as all children are different. It is usually wise to start preparations at least one year ahead of exams, but many people start to tutor their children at the beginning of Year 5.

Warning! Reserve a tutor

If you do choose to have a tutor, get your name on a list for a tutor well ahead of time – in some cases when your child is in Year 2 or 3. Good tutors have waiting lists and by the time you need one, it may be too late to get one!

HOW TO FIND A TUTOR

Good tutors are worth their weight in gold. The best type of tutor is one that is personally recommended to you and one that is familiar with the entrance school requirements. Speak to other parents or parents of children who are in older classes and spread the word that you are on the lookout for a good tutor. Also check with your school's head teacher or secretary – sometimes they have lists of good tutors with successful track records. You can also ask other schools in the area for recommendations. If you choose to use a tutoring agency, make sure it is reputable and established and is a CRB-registered body.

A crucial aspect of tutoring is that your child develops a positive working relationship with their tutor, one which will result in them growing in confidence and knowing what to expect when the exams come.

TUTOR HOMEWORK

How much homework a tutor gives a child will often depend on what the child can cope with and how old they are. Some children start tutoring in Year 3 or 4 and are given homework to help set the routine for later and consolidate things done in lessons rather than preparation for the 11+ exam.

A checklist of questions to ask a tutor

▶ *How long have they been teaching/tutoring?*
▶ *What schools do they prepare their pupils for?*
▶ *How much do they charge?*
▶ *How much homework do they set a week?*
▶ *What approach do they use for preparing their pupils to sit exams?*
▶ *When do they give feedback to parents?*
▶ *Can they give you a contact number of another parent whose child they tutor as a reference?*

The best way to revise

Different children revise in different ways, but in most cases the best bet is to set out a revision plan. Make sure your child has space and quiet to revise, as well as plenty of chill-out time, so that revision does not become too onerous.

Revision rules

1   *Decide how much work needs to be covered – how many practice papers and essays need to be written. Then establish how much time your child has available between now and the exams, and draw up a realistic timetable.*

(Contd)

2 *Stick to this timetable! That way you and your child can keep track of how much work they have done and what they have left to cover.*

3 *Choose a place in the house for your child to revise where they won't be distracted.*

4 *Make other members of the family aware of the fact that your revising child needs some peace and quiet during this time – if need be, put up some 'Keep out' or 'Be quiet' signs around the house.*

5 *Encourage your child to switch revision between subjects to avoid becoming bored of a single topic.*

6 *Ensure your child has plenty of wind-down time between revision sessions – too much work may lead to burnout.*

7 *Avoid comparing your child's abilities and exam preparation with your friends' children. Everyone approaches revision in different ways, so just make sure you've chosen the method that works best for your child.*

8 *Remember revision is just that – it's about seeing something again and refreshing your knowledge. It's not about new work. If your child has worked at a steady pace throughout the year, revision should be relatively straightforward.*

Expert opinion: tutoring

'The tradition of children attending their local primary school then, as a matter of course, continuing to their local secondary school, has almost been lost in some parts of London. Demand for state and fee-paying selective school places has increased, which in turn has led to a sharp rise in demand for entrance exam tutoring, as parents recognize they must make provision and give their children the best possible chance of successfully achieving entry into the secondary school of their choice. My dedication to preparing and supporting parents and children for secondary entrance exams is driven by a deep understanding of the frustration and resentment that many experience at having to go through this process in the first place.

What does a thorough preparation consist of? Whether a tutor is employed, or you decide to do it yourself, you will need to allow a period of approximately eighteen months to two years beforehand to ensure that comprehensive coverage of the curriculum takes place without cramming. That means the appropriate maths and English are being taught and that the students attain the correct levels. Levels are confusing, as selective secondary schools have their own ranges of levels to be achieved for successful entry and this is complicated by the annual changes that may take place due to that cohort's performance. Some years I have known children to achieve places who were borderline and the next year children who were well within the acceptance range be rejected. These are circumstances that are out of our control.

Tutoring services provide individual and group tutoring for entrance exam preparation. Let's look at group tutoring first; there are several reasons for this offering. I think the concept of children working together is extremely motivating, and this has proved to be the case. It's a more economic option with the added bonus of children pooling ideas and supporting each other. I have found children very motivated, displaying outstanding performance improvements by the experience and the comradeship that forms throughout the tutoring period. The presence of refreshments also works wonders. My fears that children may become competitive have been unfounded, in fact often quite the opposite dynamic results: a sense of "We're all in it together" seems to prevail as the children begin to take individual responsibility for their learning, share their problems and eventually achieve places.

Is group tutoring suitable for all children? No, I don't think it is. Factors need to be taken into consideration. For example, the child's starting point: is there a lot of curriculum coverage missing? In which case, they may require more intense individual work. If there are conceptual difficulties, concentration issues or special needs such as dyslexia, then individual work would be preferable. In some cases, parents have combined a base of group tutoring with some individual work when necessary.

(Contd)

At this point, I must take us back to the starting point. Before making a decision to individually tutor, group tutor or not at all, how will you know if your child is suitable? Often an appointment with your child's teacher or head teacher will clarify the matter. This meeting should ideally take place at the beginning of Year 5, when there is still enough time to ensure complete curriculum coverage takes place in a non-stressful manner. Cramming in the autumn term of Year 6 is not advisable and besides putting unnecessary strain on your child and family, it also lacks the deeper embedded understanding and the learning is fragile rather than enjoyed, practised and secure.

If your head teacher is not forthcoming, then an independent assessment would be money well spent. Having your child assessed by a professional will provide valuable information on suitability and give recommendations regarding areas to be covered and possible schools. Who to use? That's a difficult question to answer. Some tutors are qualified to do assessments. Educational psychologists are appropriate, although their costs tend to be greater due to their range of expertise. Having the right person to assess your child and thoroughly researching this will pay dividends in the long term, as it may be on the basis of their advice that your decision to tutor is made. Sometimes, the assessment results will bring up information you were not expecting to hear, such as your child may not be suitable for selection to the school of your choice; however I would argue that this too is valuable advice as now you can channel your energies and tutoring (if appropriate), into finding the most suitable option for where your child will be happiest and thrive.

Tutoring can benefit both children and parents. From the child's point of view, it provides personal support and an increased sense of self-worth as successful learning takes place in an environment of honesty, confronting challenge and coping with 'failure' and difficulties – these are the most common stumbling blocks and barriers to progress. For parents, tutoring provides a valuable support system that will lead and guide your child's learning and attitude during the entrance exam period which may last several years, or months, depending on the child's requirements and recommendations from assessment. A good tutor will be available to answer your questions and provide advice and support, not just during tutoring sessions but at other times as well, such as when the child is having difficulty with homework, or having behavioural problems.

So if you're thinking of tutoring, do your research and homework early enough to find and put your name down with the right tutor. You can always cancel your place nearer the time. The demand is so great in Years 5 and 6, that most tutors of the appropriate calibre are completely oversubscribed and would welcome an extra space coming available, should you decided not to proceed.'

Lorrae Jaderberg Shall, educational consultant

Preparing for entrance exams

'Preparing for secondary school entrance exams can be very stressful for both parents and children. Although tuition is extremely beneficial, there are several ways that you as a parent can help alleviate this pressure.

Firstly, you can make the process easier if you start preparing your child from a young age: introducing a good work routine at home is an important foundation. This should not be forced, simply encourage your child to work in a quiet environment, for short periods of time, on a regular basis. Instilling this discipline at an early age will help with future studying. To encourage your child's enthusiasm for learning, try to vary the type of work you set. Activity books, puzzles and brainteasers are examples of stimulating materials, which can help make learning fun. You could also use workbooks such as Bond Assessment Papers. These are age-specific and consist of maths, English, verbal reasoning and non-verbal reasoning. The maths and English papers are in line with the National Curriculum as well as the National Numeracy and Literacy Strategies. These can therefore be used as a guideline to monitor your child's progress. As verbal and non-verbal reasoning are not part of the National Curriculum, introducing these papers at a young age is useful, as they form part of the 11+ exams.

(Contd)

Although you should try to challenge your child, make sure you also set work that is achievable to help build confidence and maintain interest. Be conscious to praise your child's efforts irrespective of how well he/she does with the tasks you set. If you are not sure of the best way to explain certain concepts, you could ask a class teacher for help. Most teachers would be happy to guide you on how to approach the topic.

You can also help prepare by broadening your child's general knowledge and awareness of current affairs. Reading interesting newspaper articles and regularly watching the news, quiz programmes and documentaries are all beneficial. Family trips to the zoo, safari parks, museums and the theatre can be both fun and educational. Encourage your child to do extra-curricular activities such as sports, drama or playing a musical instrument. Not only are these enjoyable but should your child be invited for an interview, it is good to show that he/she has diverse interests. However, children need time to rest, so be careful not to overdo the activities.

Reading is vital. Stories will help develop vocabulary and imagination, which are essential for creative writing. Consider a variety of reading material, such as magazines, advertisements, leaflets and letters. To broaden your child's vocabulary, you should pay attention to the type of language you use in everyday discussions. Be mindful to ask open-ended questions, instead of questions resulting in a "Yes" or "No" answer. For example: What do you think of…? Why do you think that…? What would happen if…? This method of questioning will also encourage your child to be inquisitive. Have discussions with your child on topical issues and ask thought-provoking questions, encouraging him/her to share and express opinions succinctly, using vocabulary precisely. The earlier you start this dialogue, the better.

You can improve your child's mathematical skills by explaining how to apply them to real-life situations. When shopping, you can ask your child to calculate the total bill for the items you are purchasing and the amount of change you will receive. When cooking, you can ask your child to help with weighing out the ingredients and converting measurements. It is a good idea to think of ways to reinforce topics covered in school by applying them at home.

It is imperative that children practise times tables, as these are an essential tool for answering a variety of maths questions in the exams. A lack of this knowledge can lead to incorrect answers, giving the impression that topics are not understood. Your child could recite these at night before going to bed or whilst travelling to school. In order to avoid monotony try to make this as fun as possible, by introducing incentives and offering rewards.

As your child approaches Year 5, you may require tuition to help prepare for secondary school entrance exams. You should contact the tutor of your choice well in advance, as some tutors reserve places for children from as early as Year 2. Even the brightest children will need guidance with exam technique and preparation. You should also be aware that some entrance exams include maths topics that are not taught in school as part of the key stage 2 National Curriculum. Your child will need to cover these new topics to ensure that he/she is fully prepared.

You may decide to have your child tutored at a younger age if he/she is struggling to keep up with class work at school. Similarly, if your child is identified as having special educational needs, seeking help early really makes a difference. With the right guidance, your child can learn strategies to deal with these issues. In some cases, secondary schools will make provisions for children with specific learning difficulties when they sit the entrance exams.

Tuition for the 11+ exams should not be about getting your child into a particular school but into a suitable school where your child can be happy and reach his/her full potential. With training, children can get into schools that are not suitable for them, which can have a negative effect long-term. The head teacher at your child's school and/or tutor, who will have assessed your child, can advise you on the best options available. It is important to visit those schools you are interested in; this will help you make an informed decision.

(Contd)

If you are realistic and choose appropriate schools, you can ease the pressure for both yourself and your child.

Whether your child is tutored or not, he/she should work at a constant pace when preparing for the exams. As the time draws closer, avoid a sudden increase in the amount of work that is being done, as this will put unnecessary pressure on your child. Remember to talk about things other than the exams and continue to make time for fun activities.

Incorporating learning into your child's routine in a simple and fun way can be both enjoyable and rewarding. Following these practices will ensure your child is better prepared for the secondary school entrance exams and will provide a good foundation for his/her future education.'

Alison Hanouka, experienced tutor

Frequently asked questions

Where can I get hold of past papers?

That depends. Some schools, who commission an exam board to write the 11+ papers, will not distribute past papers. You can get hold of general example papers written by the exam boards which can be bought from leading bookstores. For those schools that set their own papers, they will often send out copies of past papers, as will schools that sit the Common Entrance Exam. Some schools sell past exam papers at their school open days. Assessment companies such as GL Assessment do not liaise directly with parents.

If my child fails the 11+ can they retake it at a later date?

Not unless the school also offers a 12+ or 13+ exam.

Can I get away with not hiring a tutor?

Yes. Many pupils pass without ever having to use a tutor. However, it is important that your child is familiar with the types of questions they will encounter at the 11+ exams, as these are rarely taught at school. Therefore you should make sure your child has completed practice papers.

Why are there so few practice materials?
While it is helpful to know what the tests look like and be familiar with the types of questions in the tests, schools do not want children to be so practised that the tests will not be a true reflection of their actual ability. Therefore, the number of practice papers available on the market to buy is relatively limited.

Exam preparation

▶ Don't 'hot house' your child. If you do, they will be unable to cope at secondary school. If you tutor above a child's natural level of capability for any exam, they could have an unhappy time when joining the school and their confidence may drop.
▶ Play with your child. Different types of games are valuable for different reasons. Encourage your child to play electronic or board games that require tactical thinking and rapid reactions. Also suggest they play games, like sudoku or card games, which will practise maths skills. Word games will increase your child's vocabulary, as will puzzles and crosswords. Solving brainteasers and riddles will also keep their mind active for hours!
▶ Buy a good dictionary and thesaurus.
▶ Encourage your child to read – this is the best way to increase their vocabulary. Get a library card – and use it.
▶ Practise times tables at every available opportunity.
▶ Take every possible opportunity to show your child practical ways of applying their maths skills to real-life situations, such as shopping or cooking.
▶ Encourage your child to tell you synonyms and antonyms for words.
▶ Revise prefixes, suffixes, word roots, antonyms and compound words.
▶ Give your child both an analogue and digital watch/clock so they are experienced with both ways of telling the time.

(Contd)

- ▶ *Write your own dictionary of maths words – and use it regularly for quick reference and revision. Important words to include are: properties of triangles, names of 2D and 3D shapes, an understanding and examples of square numbers, prime numbers, factors, multiples, range, mean, median and mode numbers.*
- ▶ *Remind your child that in maths they like to use 'posh' words, but they are not to be feared! If asked to 'translate' a shape, that simply means 'move'. If asked to draw a 'regular' shape, that means all the sides are equal, and so on.*
- ▶ *Encourage your child to take mathematical short cuts, for example: memorizing a poem to know how many days there are in each month; using their fingers to 'cheat' when calculating the 9-times table.*

10 THINGS TO REMEMBER

1 *The best way to prepare for the 11+ is by giving your child plenty of time to practise.*

2 *Research the different types of exams that the schools will set – these can change year on year.*

3 *Before entering your child for any exam, make sure you are aware of their academic ability and potential, and ensure that the school they are sitting the exam for is a realistic possibility.*

4 *Most exams papers test maths, English comprehension and English writing. Some will also test verbal and non-verbal reasoning.*

5 *Only private schools interview children. State selective schools are no longer allowed to interview children – places are allocated solely on exam scores.*

6 *Some schools examine in two stages, starting with verbal reasoning and non-verbal reasoning. Other schools test everything all in one go.*

7 *Practice papers, available at leading bookstores, and past school papers which can be available on the school's website, are very valuable exam preparation.*

8 *Tutors are a useful way to support your child through their examination preparation, but they are not essential. It is possible to prepare your child successfully without using a tutor.*

9 *If you decide to hire a tutor make sure they are fully CRB checked and have a proven track record.*

10 *A helpful way to support your child's revision is by getting them to write a revision plan.*

6

Success at school interviews

In this chapter you will learn:
- *which types of school interview children and which don't*
- *about the different types of interview*
- *how to improve your child's chances of impressing at interview*
- *likely questions that may come up at interview.*

The thought of an interview can be very distressing – for adults, as well as children. What if they don't like me? What if I say the wrong thing? It's hard not to take the potential rejection personally. The key to a successful school interview is to think about what it is they will be looking for and how you can prepare your child in advance to show themselves in the best possible light.

That is not to say that you should over-prepare your child – you still will want them to be themselves. Giving them set answers to say that do not reflect their real thoughts, feelings and strengths will lead to an unhappy child if they were to be offered a place under false pretences. Be honest... but be ready!

Which types of school interview children and which don't?

Since September 2008, state schools are no longer allowed to interview children as part of their selection process. The School

Admissions Code has banned the use of interviews, except for assessing suitability for boarding at boarding schools and for religious-based schools where it is currently permissible for an interview to take place in order to assess religious commitment. For all other reasons it is unlawful to interview children for school places in the state sector. This is also the case for state selective schools. They rely solely on the academic results of the tests as the basis on which to offer places.

Private schools are different; they usually do interview the children for Year 7, and wait for it... sometimes they interview the parents too. This will vary from school to school. It is important to find out ahead of time what the interview procedure is for your chosen school. In addition, many private schools ask for a primary school reference for your child and it is often their policy to offer places based on the whole picture created by all three factors – academic ability, school references and interview performance – in the belief that this will be a true gauge of a candidate's potential.

Why interview the child?

The interview is a test of your child's personality and sociability and an opportunity for the senior teachers present to ask questions about your child's hobbies, interests and strengths. It is an opportunity to decide if your child will fit in with and complement both the culture and ethos of the school, and the group of children the school is bringing together in the new year group.

The different types of interview

Some private schools automatically interview all their candidates, whereas others only interview those who are successful in the exam. While it is often your child's performance in the exam which is the most important deciding factor, an interview can still play a significant role.

Interview structures vary: sometimes your child will be interviewed individually, sometimes in pairs and, increasingly these days, in groups. Schools will regularly review their interview style, so don't assume it will stay the same from year to year. Some schools give the children two interviews: individually and then in pairs to give pupils further opportunity to give evidence of their strengths – not only in the academic field, but also in other areas where they might offer a contribution to the wider life of the school. Sometimes both interviews occur on the same day, sometimes on different days. Schools regularly state no specific preparation is required or expected for the interview.

Insight

I have found over the last few years that fewer interviews are individual these days – more are in pairs or groups. The reason for this is to see how a child interacts with others and whether their social style will be compatible with the ethos of the school.

INDIVIDUAL AND PAIRED INTERVIEWS

Interviews are an opportunity for children to make themselves as interesting and interested as possible. It is a chance for them to talk about themselves and show they can engage in conversation and can communicate their opinions. It is also an opportunity for schools to assess each child's 'teachability' and his or her likely overall contribution to the school.

Schools will go about this in many different ways, often involving direct questions as well as mini-tasks.

Popular tasks may involve asking your child to respond to a piece of text, usually verse or prose. This task tests their verbal comprehension. Sometimes the candidate is asked to actually read the text aloud; this will also be used to judge the degree of confidence that the pupil shows in reading for an audience. Another task might be to give your child a picture as a stimulus for discussion. Alternatively, they might be given a maths task to complete. It is also quite common to be asked to bring along schoolbooks and sometimes certificates or awards from 'out of school' activities. Sometimes they may be asked to bring in an object. The purpose remains the same: to establish whether your child has the confidence and ability to communicate successfully.

GROUP INTERVIEWS

The purpose of a group interview is to find out the social skills of the children and how they interact and respond to each other. Who are the leaders and followers? How well do they listen to the teacher and listen to each other? How much prompting do they need with the task? Observing this group dynamic will give the school plenty of information on the style of learning favoured by these candidates and will allow them to make decisions about each child's suitability to the school. Group interviews are usually no more than six children and after an initial introductory activity, the children will probably be given a task to complete together. This may be to discuss an object, solve a maths problem or even perform a science experiment. It may be that they are given a list of things and asked to prioritize them in order of importance. It will often involve reasoning and candidates offering opinions. Possibilities are endless and each year schools become more and more creative – but the success criteria remain the same.

Warning! Interview assumption

Don't assume that, because your child has been called back for an interview, they are likely to be offered a place. For example, it is not unusual for 500 children to sit for a private school with 100 places, with as many as 300 children being called back for an interview.

Expert opinion: interview tips

▶ '"Be yourself" is tip number one.
▶ Tip number two is: do not regurgitate parrot-fashion language and concepts beyond your years.
▶ Tip number three: read and read and read fiction, non-fiction and newspaper articles.
▶ Typically explored at interview will be English, mathematics and general knowledge or interests; new concepts may be taught, your interests explored; do be genuinely enthusiastic!
▶ Expect an individual interview and a group interview; this can be very telling in terms of interaction with others.
▶ All schools that value relationships will make time for parents to be seen by the head or deputies and they should insist on a private interview.
▶ The best schools are looking for genuine academic curiosity, allied to teachability, empathy with and sensitivity towards others and a developed or developing interest in some area of music, drama, community service and sport.'

Peter Hamilton, Head teacher of Haberdashers' Aske's Boys' School,
a boys' private secondary school in Elstree

'It is important to get a balance between preparing your child, so that she feels confident, yet not over-preparing her so that her answers lack spontaneity. The head teacher or interviewer is looking for an articulate child who can give a positive impression and offer intelligent and thoughtful answers.

I invite the parents to come into my office together with their daughter and spend a few minutes explaining what is going to happen. I want to take some of the mystery out of the process and offer some reassurance to both the parents and their daughter at the same time. The pupil is then interviewed by a senior colleague of mine and I take the time to talk to the parents and let them ask me anything about the school that they want. I generally make a joke to the child when she is on her way out of my office, that her Mummy and Daddy are interviewing me, while she is having her interview and I am far more likely to be interrogated! That tends to produce a giggle from the pupil.

The pupil, meanwhile, has a gentle interview in which she is asked about her interests and hobbies. Generally we ask what books she has read recently and get her to comment on what she liked/disliked about it. She is then invited to talk about her hobbies, the musical instruments she plays, whether she has a position of responsibility in her school. This is guided by the interviewer. We then show her a painting and ask her to describe what is going on and again to offer her opinion about it. There is no right or wrong answer; again it is just an opportunity to demonstrate that she has a view and can talk about something with interest. After that we ask her to do some mental maths, generally using a Year 6 mental maths paper that she should be familiar with, and ask her to work out the answers to some questions. We are not trying to catch her out, just to see how she works in a different setting. Time is then given to some general questions and asking her what she would like to ask as well. Meanwhile, I am in my office, being interrogated by the parents, which is usually a much more gruelling interview than their daughter is having!

It is important for parents to be aware that an interview is a two-way process and I strongly believe it is an additional way for parents, together with their daughters, to decide whether they still want to go to the school. Once the offers are out, if you are still not sure, I would suggest going back to visit the school for another tour around or ask if it is possible to meet some of the pupils or spend some time in the Year 6 or 7 class. Schools should be amenable to this as they should want to help you make an informed decision.'

Jo Ebner, Head teacher of The Royal School, a girls' private secondary school in Hampstead, London

How to improve your child's chances of impressing at interview

Never assume you know what the interviewer is looking for. Many parents think that if their child is confident and articulate, they will have a better chance of passing the interview than a child who is shy and quiet. This may be the case but does depend on what each school is looking for: they will want a good mix of personality types in each class and too many dominant, opinionated children will not be conducive to learning! They will be looking to find the perfect balance of movers, shakers and quieter children.

Insight

In my experience, offers of good school places are given to the quiet children as well as the loud ones. Don't forget that the interview is only one third of the information given to these secondary schools about your child – they will also consider their exam performance and the report from their primary school. All three pieces of information will help them decide whether they feel their school is the right place for your child.

Interview pointers for children

▶ *Don't be late for your interview – always try to get there a few minutes early.*
▶ *Treat other people you encounter with courtesy and respect. You never know if their opinions of you might be asked before making decisions. This is particularly the case for members of staff who will take the children to and from the interview room.*
▶ *Stand/sit tall – don't look at the floor.*
▶ *Dress smartly and look neat and tidy.*
▶ *No fiddling or fidgeting – keep hands on laps.*
▶ *Sit with your back on the back of the seat so you don't slouch.*
▶ *Sit in an open position – not crossing legs or arms.*
▶ *Smile and enjoy the conversation.*
▶ *Don't be afraid to ask for clarification on any difficult questions asked.*
▶ *Listen carefully to all questions and take your time to respond.*
▶ *Respond to questions and back up your answers about yourself with specific examples whenever possible.*
▶ *Always sound positive and enthusiastic about your studies but also about life in general.*

Expert opinion: interviews

'The most successful interviews cannot be prepared for. Despite that, untold man and woman hours every year are put in to preparing children for interviews, from two sources – their parents, and their school or tutors. Parents do it because they feel responsible for their child, and guilty if they don't. One head tells the story of a distraught mum asking the school's PA if she could be moved to another waiting room. The other mum in the room had prepared 30 questions she thought her child might be asked, written three-line answers for each one and had made the child learn them all. She was putting him through his memory test as they waited for interview, and the other mum was in tears because she hadn't done any of this. Some stories have a happy ending: the rehearsed child was turned down, the unrehearsed one snapped up.

Schools can also cram children, seeing the child's success or failure as reflecting their own. Yet this preparation can do more harm than good. Firstly, the rehearsed child can be completely thrown if they are not asked the questions they have been told to expect. Secondly, schools know some children are rehearsed for interviews, and have to stifle a collective sigh when the same old current affairs issues trip off a child's tongue, a child who has clearly never read a newspaper in their life. Similarly with "What have you read recently?" – a question guaranteed to produce the equivalent of a bad choice of music in *Desert Island Discs* – where the person

(Contd)

recites a list, not of what they like, but what they think the listener/interviewer will be impressed by.

What goes down really well in an interview is what is fresh, unrehearsed and natural. Any good interviewer knows how to divert the child's thoughts down an unrehearsed channel, and see if they run with it. Reading a poem and asking the child what she thinks of when someone says the word "flower"; stopping the flow of who has just been elected president and asking, "What would you do if you were president of the United States?", or interrupting gently the praise of Harry Potter and saying, "Personally, I think Harry's parents sound as if they were pretty horrible" quickly tests if a child can think on his or her feet. If you want to prepare your child for an interview, talk to them every day; encourage them to read anything legal; ration computer and TV time; take them out for long walks. Apart from the computers and TV, that advice hasn't changed in a good few thousand years.'

Jenny Stephen, Headmistress at South Hampstead High School,
a girls' private secondary school in London

Pupil case study 1: interviews

'I applied to St Marylebone, Westminster (selective Church state school), and four other schools in the private North London Consortium: City, Channing, Francis Holland and South Hampstead. Parliament Hill was my local state school and my only guaranteed place, as I was in the catchment area. The Marylebone exam was on a Saturday in October after which some girls were invited back for interviews. As I was living outside of Westminster, I could only apply for a music scholarship so was only given a music audition (not a general interview). I was not particularly scared, as this was not my first choice. However it was my first audition and it was good practice for all the others.

The first two Fridays in January were the two North London Consortium exams. Only Francis Holland called everyone back for an interview. Coming from a state school, I was given no preparation for the exam so I had to have a tutor for a year and a term. She taught me maths and English for an hour a week and she made me feel comfortable and prepared when I went into the exam. I think it is unfair on the child if she/he has to do lots of exams. They are exhausting and stressful.

They all asked me to come back for an interview several weeks later. My mum and dad prepared me for the interviews by asking me questions they thought might come up. These included current affairs, my interests, what I want to be when I grow up, what books I had read recently, and so on, so that it would all be fresh in my mind. They also took me to galleries, exhibitions and the theatre. I have been going to art galleries regularly since I was a kid so I was used to talking about art. They showed me a picture and asked me what I thought about it in two interviews. In the end I was not asked any questions about current affairs however many of my friends were. My parents told me to greet the interviewer by shaking their hand and looking them straight in the eye.

Channing was the only school that interviewed me with another girl. I found it very off-putting sharing the interview with another girl because you didn't know if you were talking too much or too little. I was given a poem to talk about and two paintings to compare. I was also asked general questions about my hobbies.

At South Hampstead, again I was given a photo of a painting which I had by chance seen in a gallery in New York! I was asked to talk about it and imagine a scenario to go with it. I also had a long discussion about books and authors.

For City, I was given mental maths questions. I was again given a poem to discuss. My sister was asked in her interview for City, "If you are walking in the countryside and you come to a crossroads, with one path leading down into the valley and one leading up the mountain, which path would you take and why?"

My final interview was Francis Holland and this was with the headmistress. We had a very long chat about my last holiday, a national art competition I had won (which she must have read from my primary school reference), what I wanted to be when I grew up, how my dad became a filmmaker and which school out of the ones I had applied to, did I really want to go to.

(Contd)

The one thing about all the interviews was they were very friendly and relaxed. I was not very nervous. Nobody was trying to trick me or catch me out. My best advice would be: be yourself, volunteer information (no "Yes/No" answers) and look them straight in the eye.

I was lucky, in that all the schools I applied to offered me a place, and I was awarded the music scholarship at St Marylebone.'

Coco (Year 8)

Pupil case study 2: interviews

'I took my interviews at the end of January and early February, following on from the three exams I had sat a couple of weeks previously. I was nervous because I am very shy and quiet but my tutor and mum helped me, and so did my mum's friend who is a drama teacher. We practised questions that might come up such as, "What hobbies do you have?" or "What do think about what's going on in the news this week?" I did not "learn" the correct answers; I simply practised the way I wanted to answer these questions from my own point of view.

For some interviews I was on my own, for one I was with another girl. Luckily for me, they asked a lot of questions that I had practised, so I knew the way I wanted to answer the questions. One thing that most schools do is give you a picture or poem and ask you to describe it in your own words. My advice is: don't over-prepare. A school is looking for a child that is natural, not a child that is perfect: just be yourself. I am now in Year 7 and loving my new school.'

Daisy (Year 7)

Likely questions that may come up at interview

While the following list of questions and 'openers' is by no means exhaustive, it does represent questions that often recur during the interview process.

- *Why have you chosen this school?*
- *Is it your first choice?*
- *Tell me about your family.*
- *Tell me about the area in which you live.*
- *What is your favourite place?*
- *Tell me about your school. What do you like best about your school?*
- *What would you change about your school?*
- *What are your hobbies? What do you do in your spare time?*
- *What are your strengths and weaknesses?*
- *How do you feel you would contribute to the life of this school?*
- *What do you like about yourself?*
- *Who do you most admire and why?*
- *What have you done that you are most proud of?*
- *If you were prime minister, what would you do?*
- *How do you hear about the news?*
- *What is your favourite TV programme?*
- *What would a teacher say about you?*
- *Tell me about a book you have read; what are you currently reading?*
- *What author would you recommend and why?*
- *What is your knowledge and understanding of a current affairs story that has recently been in the news – and what is your opinion?*

Take care with some of these answers. You will want your child to celebrate their strengths without appearing pompous or self-absorbed. You will also want their weaknesses not to be too bad, for example a useful weakness to have would be impatience, as your child can spin this into a positive – a desire to complete things quickly. Schools are looking to see if your child can articulate their opinions and draw intelligent conclusions.

Insight

I found it useful to role-play these interviews with my daughter. I never gave her answers, but wanted to give her time to think about what her responses would be and to refine her answer for the real thing. All secondary school teachers state that they can tell if a child's answer is not their own.

Expert opinion: interview preparation

'An interview is an opportunity. It is your child's opportunity to let the person interviewing them discover as much about them as possible. The interviewer is on their side and will want to get to know them. It's their chance to show who they are and what they can do. What would they like the school to know about them? They should think about their hobbies and interests but also think about the kind of person they are: What would their family say are their best qualities? What would their best friend or favourite teacher say?

It's good to have opinions too. What do they think about what is on the news? Do they have any ideas about how they would run the country if they had the chance? Having an opinion means that they can see the big picture and are aware of what's going on around them.

Before they go to their interview, encourage your child to give thought to these areas, so they can let the school know that they're interested in them, too. Encourage them to have questions to ask at the interview to show that they are interested in the school.'

Eloise Jacobs, Speech and Drama teacher and public speaking coach

Parent interviews

Parent interviews are often very informal and a chance for you to ask the head teacher questions about the school. It should also be seen as an opportunity for you to 'sell' your child. During interviews, schools may also want to find out how serious your application is, by asking if you would accept the place if offered. Many schools do not refer to their meeting with parents as interviews – merely an opportunity to meet each other and talk about the school. Don't be fooled… they are making judgements about you and your child, while discussing the pros and cons of the new drama department!

You can plan and practise for months and months, but just as with an examination, you can't guarantee what questions will come up and you might find your child will be asked a question you had not anticipated. Don't worry – encourage your child to keep their head clear and answer the question as best they can.

Interview preparation

▶ *Don't assume interview styles stay the same for each school year after year; they change them regularly!*
▶ *Don't assume each school is looking for just one type of child – they will be looking to create a balance of personalities.*
▶ *Encourage your child to recognize their strengths and weaknesses and be able to express them articulately.*

(Contd)

- ▶ *Many people are uncomfortable with direct eye contact for long periods of time. If this is the case with your child, suggest they look at the person's forehead as well as their eyes. As long as your child does not look bored or distracted by looking around the room, eye contact does not need to be ongoing throughout the whole interview.*
- ▶ *If a child does not know an answer, it is better to admit it than guess – it shows honesty and confidence.*
- ▶ *Encourage your child to suggest their own answers to questions, rather than rehearse 'off pat' your set answers. Where they have learnt a 'model' answer, make sure they can expand upon it: for example, if they are concerned about global warming, they need to be able to explain why!*

10 THINGS TO REMEMBER

1 *Only private schools interview their prospective students.*

2 *Sometimes children* and *parents can be interviewed.*

3 *Interviews can be individual, paired or in groups.*

4 *All schools would strongly advise parents not to prep their child for interview. However, discussing the interview and possible questions in order to allow your child to be slightly more prepared will generally be a benefit.*

5 *When preparing children for interviews do not give them set answers. It is always obvious to the interviewer if the child has been given a set answer. Instead, encourage your child to think of their own answers to suggested questions.*

6 *Ensure your child is dressed smartly and that you have plenty of time to spare before arriving at the interview.*

7 *Encourage your child to be themselves – you never quite know what the school is looking for and each class will need a mix of different types of personalities.*

8 *If your child is uncomfortable with direct eye contact, recommend that they look at their interviewer in the direction of their forehead between the eyes. That way they look alert and interested, but not uncomfortable.*

9 *An interview should be seen as an opportunity for a child to let the person interviewing them know as much about them as possible.*

10 *Remember to tell your child that the person doing the interviewing can be as nervous as the child.*

7

Results

In this chapter you will learn:
* *when to expect the results*
* *how to identify and cope with exam and results stress*
* *what to do if the worst happens*
* *about waiting list places – what to do and how to increase your child's chances.*

Waiting for the postman to arrive to drop that all-important letter through the letterbox is something many of us can relate to. For our children, the fear and worry may be the same, although the way that schools notify their results vary and many parents are able to access decisions online or by phone. Again, this depends on local authorities and individual schools.

When to expect the results

Private schools' exams tend to be in January, with successful candidates being called back for interview at the end of January/beginning of February. Usually the exams are all taken in one go – candidates are not called back for a second exam. Results letters are usually sent out around the third week in February.

For non-selective state schools where exams are not taken, children will be offered their schools on National Offer Day, which is usually early March.

Selective state schools often have a two-stage exam process. The first one takes place in October time – usually just before or just after half-term. This exam is usually either verbal reasoning or non-verbal reasoning or both. The results are usually distributed around two weeks later – with your child being told their score and the pass mark score.

If your child's standardized score is above the pass mark, then they will be invited back for a second examination. This exam, usually in November or January will typically include maths, English comprehension and story writing. Some schools do not sit this first test until November, which means they may only find out their results a day or two before Christmas. A rejection letter is not the best Christmas present for any child, and it has the potential to ruin any parents' mulled wine and mince pies. Don't despair if your child's results aren't what you were hoping – it is very important to have a back-up plan, a plan B! If invited back for a second examination, pupils will receive their results on National Offer Day at the beginning of March through the local authority.

Expert opinion: have a plan B

'The important thing to note is that most selective schools are heavily oversubscribed and that there are sometimes more than ten applications for every place. They are popular schools and therefore demand severely outstrips supply. What that means in practice is that many very able and talented pupils do not get a place. If your child applies and is not successful, this is not a comment on his or her ability but often on the school's capacity.

There is no easy way to make sure you get the school that is right for your child. You have to make sure that you know as much as you

(Contd)

can about the range of schools on offer; beyond that, you have to be circumspect. If you are going to try for a selective school, then you also have to take the pragmatic view that you may or may not get a place and should therefore have a plan B.

Whatever school you choose, it is true to say that pupils who are curious, well-motivated and supported by their parents can do well whatever their school. The most important factors in your child's education, in the end, are you and your child. School choice is a part of education, but it is not the only part, and not even – in the long run – the most important part.'

Oliver Blond, Head teacher of The Henrietta Barnett School, a girls' state selective secondary school in North London

How to identify exam and results stress

It's perfectly natural to feel some apprehension in the run-up to the results. The anticipation of results can be a stressful time for both children and parents. Stress affects different people in different ways.

Common symptoms of stress

▶ *sleeping difficulties or difficulty waking up in the morning*
▶ *constant fatigue*
▶ *forgetfulness*
▶ *aches and pains for no apparent reason*
▶ *poor appetite*
▶ *social withdrawal*
▶ *loss of interest in activities*
▶ *increased anxiety and irritability*
▶ *mood swings*
▶ *migraines/headaches.*

Stress happens when something unpleasant happens around us and puts us in a state of strain. It can also be experienced when we are aware of a marked imbalance between what we are capable of achieving and what we need to achieve.

Stress can often be associated with exams and waiting for results. Normal levels of stress can help you work, think faster and more effectively, and improve your performance. An 'adrenalin rush' can often help you over difficult periods. However, too much stress can not only muddle your mind, it can also affect your physical health. Your desire for your child to pass their exams may become all-consuming and fear of them not being successful can be positively overwhelming. Talking to other parents and hearing how other parents are coping can also be stressful – not everyone will admit to being as nervous as you. For many, the utter lack of control over the whole process is the most stressful part.

Your child may also be feeling the pressure; they don't want to let you down and it is possible you are pushing them too hard. They may feel an element of uncertainty for the future; if they don't pass this school exam, they may feel they will go to a poor school and their future will be doomed. They will also sense your anxieties. They may be concerned about Year 7 and the changes associated with a transition to a new secondary school.

Insight

I found it a lot easier discussing my anxieties and worries with friends – you know, those moments where you fear your child will end up with no school and you will have to home tutor. These occasional bleak moments must not be allowed to fester – talk it through and a problem shared is very much a problem halved. It can be very helpful talking to someone who has been through the whole process and come out unharmed at the other end.

How to cope with the stress and anxiety of waiting for results

Like all problems, the first and most important step is to recognize that you and your child are feeling stressed. The second step is to do something about it.

How to reduce stress for you and your child

- ▶ Give yourself and your child special wind-down time. For example, relaxing in a warm bubble bath, listening to soothing music and shutting out the world for a while.
- ▶ Take time for your mind and body to relax. For example reading, meditation, hypnotherapy, dancing and yoga.
- ▶ Experiment with homeopathy – a homeopath can prescribe remedies for exam nerves after listening to the problem and considering the symptoms.
- ▶ Take time to exercise. Regular and frequent exercise is a good stress buster!
- ▶ Eat well, and eat regularly.
- ▶ Talk to your family and friends. Make time to see your mates, it will help you unwind and allow you to unburden yourself of any problems.

What to do if the worst happens

If you are a natural pessimist you will always assume the worst; it's a defence mechanism to make the reality of failure a little less painful if it actually happens. In the main, you will find that your worst fears are unfounded. Nonetheless, some children will fail entrance examinations or not be offered the state school of their choice but it's not the end of the world. Being unsuccessful doesn't make you a failure in life... although for many it may feel like it.

How to cope with exam failure and disappointment

So what happens if things don't work out as you'd hoped? Suppose you've just been told your child didn't make the grade or meet with a school's admissions criteria? Not doing as well as expected – or hoped – can be really tough for a child. It can also be tough if they feel as if they didn't meet the expectations of others, such as you, other family members or their teachers.

Your child might experience a range of feelings that could include disappointment, anger, numbness, guilt, confusion, sadness, physical sickness and hopelessness. It can be especially difficult if their friends are celebrating and are happy about their results.

Then, there's you. You need to be there to pick up the pieces – even when you feel broken! It can be very difficult encouraging your child to be positive when you are deeply disappointed.

PICKING UP THE PIECES

Deal with your child's feelings first
Your child is bound to be feeling sad and disappointed. You need to let them know you are still proud of them, that you still love them; they did their best and it was just not meant to be. Encourage your child to talk about their feelings – make sure that no one was putting unrealistic pressures and expectations on your child.

Discuss plan B with them in a positive way. You will have put alternative choices on your CAF and/or applied to other private schools. Ensure that all the schools your child has applied for are seen in a favourable light – even if you do feel some are much better than others. If the worst-case scenario happens, you do not want to be contradicting previously unfavourable things you said about the school which is now your child's only option. It's possible that your child will be very happy at this school.

Parent case study

'At the beginning of Year 6 I got caught up in the frenzy of visiting secondary school open evenings and became an expert at gleaning information and taking notes about prospective schools. I saw a fair spectrum of schools from selective to non-selective and Christian-based faith schools. I studied Ofsted reports, school brochures and previous statistics in relation to limited catchment areas. I made appointments to consult our primary school head teacher and the staff with a view to remaining realistic about our options in relation to our son's academic progress. Somewhat unwisely I listened to the views of other parents who were often very vocal about schools that they had heard were not good schools. Finally – and in a blind panic with only a few weeks between school visits and the entry date for application forms – we made our choices. At the top of the list was a Catholic non-selective boys' school, followed by a heavily oversubscribed selective mixed school and finally, our third and last choice, the local non-selective boys' school.

We were resigned to using our 'faith card' as a means of gaining an advantageous entry to the Catholic school at the top of our list. As a back-up we pressed our son into sitting the entrance exam for the selective school in order to prove to him that we had faith in his abilities should he query this at a later stage. Finally and as a "last resort", which is what I heard from another parent, we listed the local school as a realistic option, knowing that we would be guaranteed a place if all else failed. Well, it did fail!

Much to our surprise and disappointment we were turned down by our first choice, the Catholic school, due to oversubscription with sibling preference playing a large part and the resultant reduction in the catchment area. We were also rejected by our second choice, the selective school, on the basis that our son was unable to pass the entrance exam. Left with no choice in this lottery system of secondary school applications we were duty bound to accept a place for our son at the local school.

The following summer, having suffered a failed appeal to the Catholic school, I begrudgingly bought a uniform for our son to attend the local school. I recall being positively obstructive with my negative line of questioning at an invited parent induction session. I remember asking why the school wasn't doing more to tidy its image by insisting that the children wear their uniforms properly, having observed pupils sloping to school with shirts hanging out and wearing trainers. I walked my son to school on his first day with an angry lump in my throat. Unlike me, he was stoic in his acceptance of his new school and didn't complain once, despite knowing that his closest friends were heading for either private or state selective schools. Within time we too would learn to accept this enforced placement and to embrace the benefits of our local school.

Before long we realized that we had been unjust in allowing others to taint our opinions of this school without first-hand experience. Historically the school had a good reputation, which the new headmaster was keen to uphold. The current administration has adopted a very honest approach to improving the standards of the school through better teaching practices with the well-being and achievements of the pupils at the top of the list of priorities.

In summary, we have been pleasantly surprised by the successful outcome of this school placement for our son. It was not our first choice, but it was a good choice and we should have had more faith in the system. We made unreasonably negative judgements about this school based on an old Ofsted inspection report, hearsay and selective personal observations. At the end of the day the progress of our son has been monitored effectively by a team of dedicated staff in a school keen to make every effort to invest in the next generation.

Despite every possible preparation, nobody can truly forecast whether their child will flourish in a particular school. We have been fortunate to witness our son growing from strength to strength in his academic studies with the enthusiastic support of his tutors, but this has not been as a result of our intervention with tutoring at primary

(Contd)

school level. There is no doubt that he has benefited from attending the local secondary school with a friendship base within easy access. The convenience factor of his daily walk to and from school has been immeasurable. We still hear about the discourteous and disruptive nature of some of the children at the school, but this behaviour is by no means exclusive to this school.

My advice to other parents is not to get too hung-up on the whole secondary school transfer process. Do your homework and select your schools with at least one realistic option and leave fate to play its part. Try to remain open-minded and maybe you'll be pleasantly surprised at the nurturing efforts made by the staff and the progress made by your child at the school for which they have been accepted. Stand back and let your children prove themselves and find their own niche.'

Clare, mother of Fergus (Year 7)

Deal with your feelings second

Privately, don't suppress your feelings – whether it's shock, denial, frustration or even anger – your emotions will be running high so it's important to let them out. Talking is often the most effective way of expressing yourself. You'll find that putting your feelings into words will help. Even if it's just a chance to vent, it'll clear your head so you can take stock of the choices you now face. Turn to friends, family, even your child's tutor, and take that vital first step to moving on from what feels like a disaster. Sometimes it can help to talk to someone outside the situation, such as the head teacher of your child's primary school. Challenge and reset your own expectations – sometimes it can be helpful to rethink your own expectations for your child. This may help you decide if they are realistic or not. A useful question to ask yourself might be: 'If I knew someone in a similar situation, what advice would I give to them?'

Understanding what went wrong

Think about why your child was unsuccessful. Was it always touch and go whether your child would succeed? Were they always borderline? If this is the case and they gave it their best shot then their failure might not be a huge surprise. You need to also factor in that your child might not have been happy at that school anyway.

Was it possible that your child failed the exam due to a bad exam day? Maybe they turned the page and freaked out, or simply found they revised some of the wrong things. Perhaps they answered the questions they wanted the questions to be, rather than what the questions actually asked. Perhaps their mind went blank and they panicked. If this is the case, it is important for your child to understand that it happens; people do mess up from time to time and they should not blame themselves. Perhaps nothing went wrong and your child performed really well and got great results, but sadly not high enough to be offered a place. In these circumstances, you have to accept that it is simply a case of supply and demand, with demand significantly outstripping supply.

Insight

I found it helpful to emphasize to my daughter how hard it would be to get into our local state selective school – I told her that only the top 5% would pass and admitted to her that I certainly would not have been successful! We talked about the fact that if she didn't get in it was because there were so many people applying and that it was in no way an indication of her intelligence or value to that school. I also told her that she would be an asset to any school and it would be their loss!

Waiting list places: what to do and how to increase your child's chances

A 'Yes' is an offer, a 'No' is a rejection and a 'Maybe' is a waiting place. Here's how they work.

STATE SCHOOL WAITING LISTS

The process of waiting or reserve lists varies across local authorities and also from year to year. In some cases, all admissions are handled by the local authority until around November of Year 7. After that time, if you still require a Year 7 space for your child, you will be able to contact the individual schools direct and they will send you the relevant forms and if they don't have spaces will create their own waiting list. Sometimes schools create their own waiting lists from September when the children join them in Year 7. In some boroughs the system is different, depending on the type of preferred school. Community school waiting lists are dealt with as described above, but voluntary aided and foundation schools will take over their own admissions from the borough after March's National Offer Day.

Some authorities will automatically put you on the waiting list of any schools that you ranked higher on your initial list than the school where you have been offered a place. Others invite you to request a place on the waiting list of the school you have been unsuccessful in gaining an offer for. It is quite common for children to have their name down on more than one school's waiting lists.

Candidates are ranked on the waiting list for these schools in the same order as appears in the admissions policy. No priority will be given to any candidate on the basis of the date their name was added to the list and being placed on a waiting list in no way affects your right of appeal against an unsuccessful application.

Warning! Waiting list ranking

Obviously, the higher up you are on a waiting list, the more chance you have of being given an offer. Just because you are highly ranked on a particular waiting list does not mean you will be offered a place – and conversely you can be relatively low on another waiting list and still be offered a place. Thus potentially a child on the waiting list at number three for an oversubscribed school may not ever be offered a place, whereas a child who is number 30 on the waiting list for a less popular school may be offered a place.

STATE SELECTIVE SCHOOL WAITING LISTS

Again, this varies from school to school. Many state selective schools will have a two-process entrance exam. For example, let's say 2,000 pupils apply for 180 places. Approximately 500 might be called back for the second exam. Out of these, 180 will be offered places and the remaining 320 will be put on the waiting list in exam results order. In another school, it may be that 180 places are offered and only the next 50 candidates are put on the waiting list. As you can imagine, the higher you are up the waiting list, the more likely you are to be successful and you will need to check with each school to understand the realistic chances your child will have.

PRIVATE SCHOOL WAITING LISTS

If you are offered a place on the waiting list for a private school you need to ring them up and find out how high up the list your child is and let them know if you intend to stay on the waiting list.

What to do if you need to accept one place before you have all the results

Private school offers come out before state school offers. Usually each private school will send out their offers around the same time – commonly in the same week. Each offer has a 'sell by' date; an offer will be open to your child usually for up to two weeks and then will be offered to another child who is on its waiting list. In order to secure your place, you will need to send them a deposit, which is usually a percentage – or all – of the first term's fees. This can equate to thousands of pounds. Most private schools do keep their offers open until after National Offer Day, thus allowing parents to make informed judgements based on the results of their chosen local authority school.

Where parents are left in a dilemma, is if they have been put on the waiting list for their favoured state school and also been offered a place at their back-up private school. In these circumstances, some parents may wish to accept their favourite back-up private school and then wait to find out later if their child is offered a place at their state school. They might even be waiting on the results of an appeal. If they are then offered a place at their preferred school from the state sector they can simply decline the private school offer and it will be passed to someone else. Unfortunately, they will lose their deposit. Obviously, this can be an expensive safety belt – but you have to weigh up your options and consider if it is a risk worth taking: is it worth jeopardizing or rejecting your child's private school offer and then not securing the state school of your choice?

Remember: if you are not happy with the state school that you have been offered then you have the right to appeal (see Chapter 8).

Preparing for results

▶ *Have a back-up plan in case your child does not get into the school of your choice.*

▶ *Encourage your child to think positively about all the schools you have applied for; belittling the school which they end up being offered is a difficult situation to spin into a positive.*

▶ *Make it clear to your child that if they are not successful, this is more about the fact that the school is oversubscribed than your child's ability. Lots of extremely bright children do not get offers from their first choice of school, simply because of the numbers competing.*

▶ *Be aware that you will probably find out the private school results before the state school results and you may need to consider in advance whether you will secure your private school offer as a back-up in case your preferred state school option is unsuccessful. This will mean possibly wasting quite a considerable amount of money on a deposit, but will give you peace of mind.*

10 THINGS TO REMEMBER

1 *On the whole, 11+ results for private schools come out at the end of February, and state school places are offered on National Offer Day which is in the first week of March.*

2 *The state sector will offer only one school – even if you have been accepted by a number of schools listed on your preference list.*

3 *Your local authority must only offer you your highest ranking choice where you meet the criteria.*

4 *If you are not accepted by any of your choices, the local authority will offer you a place at a school that is undersubscribed.*

5 *The private sector may make a range of offers and give you a deadline to accept or decline.*

6 *In order to secure a place in Year 7 for your child at a private school, a term's fees is usually requested in advance.*

7 *Both private schools and state schools can have waiting lists.*

8 *Be realistic about your child's chances of success and always have a back-up plan at the ready.*

9 *If you suspect your child is feeling the strain, engage in stress-busting activities.*

10 *If your child has been unsuccessful in getting into a school, explain that it is not their fault – it is more to do with the school being oversubscribed or only a very small percentage being able to get in through the examinations.*

8

How to appeal

In this chapter you will learn:
- *how the appeal system works in England, Scotland and Wales*
- *about the most commonly used grounds for an appeal*
- *how appeals differ for state selective schools*
- *what other options are available to you if your appeal is unsuccessful.*

If you did not get the state secondary school of your choice for your child then it will feel like your world has come crashing down... hard! Nonetheless you must do two things to keep yourself sane:

1 *Keep away from the competition – don't spend too much time finding out how successful other children were at getting into their chosen schools. It will only make you feel worse.*
2 *Immediately decide your next strategy.*

Most importantly, don't forget your child. It is really important that they understand that this is not their fault and that the decision is based purely on numbers. The reason why your child was not offered a place will be because the preferred school received more applications than there are places available; the children closer to their criteria are offered those places first. It is nothing personal – nothing to do with the way you look or the way you talk. Your child is simply not the best match to the admissions criteria.

The appeal system for state schools

As the phrase goes, 'If at first you don't succeed, try, try again'… or in other words, APPEAL! If you wish to challenge the decision made by your admissions authority you may do so formally by appealing against the decision. Your local authority offer letter will give you information on your right to appeal. It will explain why you have been unsuccessful and it will explain what to do next and give you a deadline to submit your appeal. By returning the appeal form within the required number of days and filling in the details asked for, you will be triggering the appeal process. Your appeal will be heard before an appeals panel whose role is simply to consider whether the school's published admissions arrangements have been properly applied. For more information, you can research the *School Admission Appeals Code of Practice (2009)* issued by the Department for Children, Schools and Families which can be found by clicking on www.dcsf.gov.uk/sacode/.

Unsuccessful applications

Your offer letter from your LEA should tell you why your application to your preferred school has not been successful. Sometimes, because of the volume of letters being sent out, LEAs will include only very general information, saying that the schools you applied for were oversubscribed and the places were filled by applicants with a higher priority than yours. This type of information does not explain in detail why your application was not successful and will be difficult for you to challenge at appeal. Therefore you should write to the admissions authority and ask for more detailed clarification as to why your application was unsuccessful.

WHO IS AT THE APPEAL AND WHAT ARE THEIR ROLES?

Appeal panels normally consist of three members, but can occasionally have five. Members are appointed by the admissions authority and can include a 'lay' member – someone without any personal experience in school management or an 'other' member – someone who has experience in education, who is acquainted with educational procedures or who is a parent of pupils at other schools. There must be a minimum of one lay member and one other member in each panel. Usually there is one lay member and two other members on a panel.

It is not essential that you attend the hearing, but it is a good idea because sometimes the panel has questions which only you can answer. Unless there are exceptional reasons, children are not invited to attend the hearing.

Another, integral member of the appeal's procedure is the clerk, who is the person with overall responsibility for the running of the appeal, though not an actual member of the panel. The clerk's key tasks are to:

- '... make the necessary administrative arrangements for hearings, including appointing panel members (unless this has been done by a separate independent appeals administrator);
- explain the basic procedure to appellants and deal with any questions they may have before the hearing (the chair or clerk, as appropriate, may deal with questions raised during the hearing);
- be an independent source of advice (or to seek appropriate advice) on procedure, on both the School Admissions and School Admission Appeals Codes of Practice, and on the law on admissions, giving any advice in the presence of all parties where practicable;
- ensure that both the appellants and the admission authority have the opportunity to present relevant facts at the hearing. The clerk's role is to assist the panel, admission authority or parents with procedure and obtaining advice where directed by the chair to do so, but not to otherwise participate in the hearing;
- record the proceedings, attendance, voting outcomes, panel decisions and reasons in such a form that the panel and clerk agree is appropriate. This record does not need to be verbatim, but must record the points raised at the hearing and make clear what view the panel took in coming to its decision about important points raised by appellants; and
- notify all parties of the panel's decision in writing' (School Admission Appeals Code of Practice (2009) paragraph 1.26).

HOW DOES THE APPEAL RUN?

The structure of the whole appeal process is quite straightforward. While there are no legal guidelines on the order of the hearings, they usually run in a similar format.

An appeal starts with an introduction and welcome by the chair member. This is the lead member who introduces everyone in the room and explains the whole proceedings. Firstly the case for the admission authority is heard. After the presenting officer is finished, they may be asked questions by the panel. The school may also send a representative, usually the head teacher or deputy head teacher, who will explain why the school cannot accept your child. If they do not attend in person they may write a report. Then it is your turn… a time for you to present your case. Next you may be asked some questions. After this, both sides are given an opportunity to sum up. Then both you and the presenting officer from the admission authority will be asked to leave the room at the same time. It is at this point that the panel deliberates and makes up its mind.

WHAT DOES THE APPEAL PANEL NEED TO DECIDE?

The appeal panel has to make three important decisions.

1 *Were the admission arrangements correctly applied in your case? Oversubscription criteria which are permissible include:*
   ▷ *'looked after' children*
   ▷ *children with special educational needs*
   ▷ *siblings*
   ▷ *social and medical needs*
   ▷ *random allocation*
   ▷ *home-to-school distance*
   ▷ *catchment areas*
   ▷ *faith-based admissions*
   ▷ *banding.*

   In the box below there is a list of all admission criteria that are strictly forbidden to be used by schools. These would be seen as an incorrect application of the admission arrangements by an appeal panel.

'2.16 In setting oversubscription criteria the admission authorities must not:

   a) *stipulate any conditions that affect the priority given to an application such as taking account of other preferences for schools made on the same application form or the type of school previously attended by the child unless those schools are named* feeder schools in accordance with paragraph 2.72. For example, by saying that priority will be given if all or some other preferences are for a school with particular characteristics (e.g. other schools are of a particular religious denomination) or on the basis that the child attended a particular type of school previously. This includes criteria often described as 'conditionality';

b) give priority to children according to the order of other schools named as preferences by their parents, including 'first preference first' arrangements;

c) give priority to children according to their parents' willingness to give practical support to the ethos of the school which includes:
   ▷ asking parents to commit themselves or their child to taking part in activities outside of normal school hours; and
   ▷ asking parents to support the school financially or in any other practical way.

d) give priority to children according to the occupational, financial or marital status of parents;

e) give priority to children according to the educational achievement or background of their parents;

f) take account of reports from previous schools about children's past behaviour, attendance, attitude or achievement;

g) discriminate against or disadvantage children with special educational needs or disabilities;

h) allocate places to relatives of former pupils of the school. A former pupil includes a sibling who will not be at the school when the younger child starts. This includes those who were attending at the time the younger sibling's application is made but will have left by the time of admission;

i) take account of the behaviour of other members of a child's family, whether good or bad, including a good or bad attendance record of other children in the same family;

j) give priority to children whose parents are current or former staff or governors or who have another connection to the school, subject to paragraph 2.18 below;

k) give priority to children according to their or their parents' particular interests, specialist knowledge or hobbies. This does not include taking account of membership of, or participation in, religious

(Contd)

2   Can the school accommodate any more pupils without causing any problems for the school?

3   Are the personal reasons that you have put forward for your child wanting to attend the school compelling enough to outweigh any prejudice that may be caused to the school? (It is possible that the addition of your child via appeal will negatively affect others – for example, if the class size rises above 30.)

Insight

I have found that many people will try to appeal as they believe the system is wrong and their child deserves a place in that particular school. Unfortunately, that is not the issue. The system may well disadvantage their child, but it all comes down to admissions criteria and if your child does not meet those criteria, fair or unfair, they will not be offered a place and the appeal will be overturned.

WHAT EVIDENCE DO YOU NEED TO BRING WITH YOU?

At least five working days before the hearing, the admissions authority should send you a copy of its statement detailing reasons why it turned you down for a place. The statement is also sent to the appeal panel. There is no statutory deadline for the submission of information about your appeal but it is good practice to submit such information as early as possible.

For an appeal to be successful, you will need to support your reasons with firm evidence. To help your case, you should enlist the help of third parties who can write supporting statements that concur with your reasons. Third parties may include council workers, social workers, psychologists, councillors or other types of professionals. For example, if you believe there are strong medical grounds as to why your child should attend a particular school, you will benefit from the written support of your GP. This needs to be as convincing as possible – perhaps including an examination or specialist's referral. The doctor needs to clearly state why your child needs to attend this particular school based on their medical knowledge of the child, rather than the emotional request of the parent.

Expert opinion: chair of admissions appeal panel

'The members of the appeals panel are independent and impartial and do not have any connection with the local education authority or with any of the schools which parents are appealing for. Most chairs of appeals panels try to make the hearing as informal as possible and try to create a pleasant atmosphere. During the general introductions, the chair also has to ask whether the parents have any objection to the panel hearing their appeal. If they know a member of the panel they must say so – the same applies to the panel member – and another appeal will be arranged.

(Contd)

Parents should also have the opportunity of putting questions to the representative from the local authority or deputy/head teacher if they attend the appeal, although in practice parents generally don't know what to ask. The panel usually ask the salient questions, for example: Are the class sizes within legal regulations? How many pupils with special educational needs (SEN) are there at the school? What is the number of pupils with English as an additional language (EAL)? The answers to these questions give the panel information as to whether prejudice will occur if another child is admitted.

If parents are appealing on the grounds of home-to-school distance, it is imperative that they tell the panel how long it will take the child to get to the allocated school – for example, two buses followed by a long walk of over an hour – versus a short ten-minute minute walk to the school they are appealing for. Whereas panels appreciate that parents like to take their child to school if possible, a child aged 11 or 12 should be able to travel on their own. At most appeals, a map is produced showing the location of the family home and school; once the school's geographic 'catchment area' is explained, parents often understand why they have not been allocated a place.

Panels do appreciate the stress that parents are under and try to be as considerate as possible.'

Shirley Bilgora, chair of admissions appeal panel, London Borough of Barnet

How do appeals differ for state selective schools?

State selective schools have only two grounds which can be used to refuse your child's application. The first reason is that your child did not pass the entrance exam and therefore your child's application will not be compatible with the school's admission arrangement. The second reason is that your child's admission would prejudice efficient use of resources or efficient education. In these circumstances, it means that your child has passed the test, but there were more successful applications than places available and other pupils had a higher priority than your child when measured against the published admission criteria.

In order to appeal successfully if your child has failed the exam, you will need to put forward reasons as to why your child did not perform to their best on the day of the test. You will stand more chance of success if the difference between your child's score and that of the pass mark is minimal. You will need to explain about any issues that may have adversely affected your child's performance when they took the exam. This could include illness or family incident such as the death of a close family member. Whatever the reason, it will be helpful if you can provide evidence to support your claim, for example a medical certificate or report from your doctor or statement from a third party explaining how the personal circumstances affected your child's performance. You will also need to give evidence that your child is able to meet the academic standards of the chosen state school. To do this, you could ask for supporting information from your child's primary school, for example: predicted end-of-key stage 2 SATs results, end-of-Year 5 QCA test results and any other method of proving your child's academic ability.

Did you know?

For the majority of parents who are unsuccessful in their secondary school application, the reason is because they live too far away from their preferred school.

The result of an appeal

The appeal decision will be made on a simple majority. After the appeal the clerk will write to the parents and the admissions authority as soon as possible after the decision is made. Some panels will ask parents to ring a phone number the next day to find out their decision. This only differs when there is a case of multiple appeals, where a number of parents are individually appealing against the decision of a particular oversubscribed school not to admit their children. In this case, a decision will not be made until all of the appeals for the same school are heard.

The decision of the panel is binding on the admissions authority. There is no further right of appeal, but if you believe that the appeals procedures were not correctly followed or you are unhappy about the way the appeal hearing was carried out, you could complain to the Local Government Ombudsman (LGO), who will investigate the case. The LGO will only rule in favour of the complainant if it is proved that there was maladministration which caused injustice.

_____

What if the appeal is unsuccessful?

Your choices are limited. You are not allowed to reapply for a place at the same school for a year unless there is a material change in your circumstances, such as a change of address or medical reasons. Ultimately you have three options:

▶ *Firstly, you can settle for another school.*
▶ *Secondly, you can accept this other school but go on the waiting list of your preferred school. Don't worry – accepting your 'settle' school will not reduce your chances on the waiting list, but it will give you a safe back-up. Then you wait... and wait.*
▶ *Thirdly, if you are not happy with any of the schools offered, then you must consider home tuition. By offering you a school, your local authority has met with their legal requirements. If you choose not to send your child to that school then it becomes your legal obligation to educate your child at home. Many choose this path, not just educating quite literally in the home, but by taking advantage of real learning places like museums, libraries, sports centres, galleries and so on to educate their children.*

Parent case study

'I moved my family abroad for a better schooling, but found myself not settling as readily as I would have liked and yearning to be back in the familiar routine of home.

So, about a year later, I returned to England, two kids in tow, with no school place. It was the secondary school place that was harder to secure. My son was now in Year 7 and most school places were full. I was in the catchment area for my local comp, but not able to gain a place there. The school my son was offered by my local authority was not one I wanted — it was right at the other end of the borough and it did not have a good reputation. And so my campaign for justice began. I rang/mailed/phoned/smoke signalled all the local schools in a bid for a better refuge for him. Meanwhile I decided to home school him. This largely consisted of home economics (cooking lunch and dinner), PE (walking in lieu of having a car at the time, and a few hefty weights, in terms of carrying my weekly shopping), social studies (a matter of observation and conversation), many field trips (having just relocated back to London, this was fun for us both) and budgeting. Life skills played a big part in his (and my) education at the time.

My son was on a waiting list for his preferred local comp and I prepared an appeal with the help of a friend who had done the same some months prior. The whole experience was fraught and nerve-racking. They 'heard' the case and, in my opinion, were extremely unsympathetic and unhelpful. I appealed on social grounds (i.e. living in a new country, needing security of old friends, travelling distance and so on). You can appeal on social and medical grounds. Put in as much detail as possible. Explain why the school is the only school for you (although you may be applying to many schools at the time); research its strengths and show your knowledge and show your interest.

I thought I had done a marvellous job, but I lost the appeal and was shocked by the result. A few weeks later however, I was overjoyed when another school that I had contacted and kept in touch with, contacted me and offered my son a place. It was just a matter of perseverance and

(Contd)

being in the right place at the right time. I did keep on ringing all the schools and I got to know some of the secretaries particularly well – my phone bill was colossal that month!

In hindsight, home schooling was fun. But I don't recommend it unless you have the time and energy. I also don't recommend giving up and sticking your child in an inappropriate school for them. It is worth hanging on and fighting your ground. Everyone wants the best for their children.

So in short, don't give up. You will live in "limbo land" while you go through the appeal and wait to hear the result; invest in some good vitamins, take up t'ai chi, light some scented candles and chant a mantra – something like, "My child is worth this stress, my child deserves a good school, my child will get the best start in life that I can give him/her."

For me, the happy ending is the stuff dreams are made of. Hopefully, my daughter will attend the same school and I will feel at ease with having done the best that I possibly can at this time in my life for my offspring. It's the least I can do for them. I am investing the time in their future (and eventually mine).'

Emily, mother of Guy (Year 7) and Emma (Year 5)

Although you're not legally required to inform your local authority when you decide to educate your child at home, it is helpful if you do so. If you are taking your child out of school to home educate them, you need to inform the school in writing.

To keep a check on the standard of education given at home, local authorities can make informal enquiries of parents who are educating their children at home. If this happens, you will need to provide evidence that your child is receiving a suitable education. This can be achieved by writing a report or providing samples of your child's work. It is possible for local authority representatives to come to your house. If the local authority considers that your child is not receiving a suitable education, it might serve a School Attendance Order.

Did you know?

▶ *You do not need to be a qualified teacher to educate your child at home.*

▶ *Your child does not have to follow the National Curriculum or take national tests, but as a parent you are required by law to ensure your child receives a full-time education suitable to their age, ability and aptitude.*

▶ *Any special educational needs your child may have must be recognized.*

▶ *You do not need to observe school hours, days or terms.*

▶ *You do not need to have a fixed timetable, nor give formal lessons.*

▶ *There are no funds directly available from central government for parents who decide to educate their children at home.*

▶ *Some local authorities provide guidance for parents, including free National Curriculum materials.*

COMMON YET NOT NECESSARILY SUCCESSFUL REASONS GIVEN AT APPEAL FOR WHY CHILDREN SHOULD GO TO THE SCHOOL FOR WHICH THEY ARE APPEALING:

▶ *The school would suit your child because it offers specialist facilities – for example music – and your child is gifted and talented in this area.*

▶ *You already have another child at the school.*

▶ *It would be difficult, from a practical reason, to get your child to another school.*

▶ *There are particular medical and social reasons why your child should go to this school.*

▶ *Religious reasons requiring your child to go to a particular school, for example single-sex.*

▶ *It is the closest school.*

▶ *The school is within walking distance.*

▶ *The school offers before- and after-school facilities.*

▶ *It has a good academic record.*

- *The school has a caring ethos.*
- *My child has friends attending the school.*
- *Most of the children in my child's school are transferring to the school.*

The appeal system for private schools

The independent sector doesn't have a formal process for appeal. In the main, your child will be unsuccessful because they did not pass the examination or others passed with higher scores. In special circumstances, you may put a case together in writing explaining why your child did not perform to their best ability in the exam – for example due to illness or upsetting personal circumstances such as divorce or death. It is then up to the school to decide how to proceed.

The appeal system in Scotland

The vast majority of Scottish LEAs use catchment areas or 'zones' to determine school places and children will usually attend their catchment school. This is called their 'designated' school. You do, however, have a right to choose a different school. To do this, you must tell your LEA what you want to do and you must put it in writing. Some authorities may provide forms, others simply ask for you to put your request in writing. Once your written request has been received the LEA will offer a place at the school of your choice unless it is oversubscribed. If you then wish to appeal, the LEA will set up an appeal committee. Each appeal committee is made up of a maximum of seven people and will run in a similar fashion to the English appeals panel. If the appeal committee agrees with the LEA's decision and dismisses your appeal, you can then appeal to the Sheriff against the appeal committee's decision.

The appeal system in Wales

The whole system of admissions and appeals in Wales is very similar to that of England. In order to fully understand any differences it is important to read the *Welsh Code of Practice* (April 1999) which sets out the requirements for school admission and appeals in Wales. In Wales, if your appeal is unsuccessful and you feel you did not receive a fair hearing, you can contact the Public Service Ombudsman for Wales.

Frequently asked questions

How long will it be before my appeal is heard?
Usually between four and six weeks from the date you send your form to the clerk of the independent panel.

Is there a deadline for me to submit my appeal?
Yes. The letter from the admissions authority will tell you the deadline for submitting your appeal.

What should I put as my reasons for appeal?
It is important that you tell the panel everything which might help them to make a decision. Give them any medical or supporting material as early as possible before the hearing.

Should I wait for the appeal before finding an alternative school?
No. You need your security in case you are unsuccessful and it will not adversely affect your appeal.

When and where is the panel hearing held?
This should be at a neutral venue and the clerk will inform you of the details at least ten clear days before the appeal hearing.

What if I am unable to attend on the day?

You should inform the clerk immediately. It is very unlikely they will delay for you. They will go ahead and review your written evidence. It should not affect your case adversely.

Who can I bring along with me to the appeal?

Legally you are allowed to take anyone along with you to the appeal. While the panel and clerk will try to make the whole process as easy as possible, it can be stressful and so having a familiar face providing you with support and encouragement can be an asset. Some parents think it wise to come to an appeal with a solicitor. This is generally not recommended as their legal knowledge is often not much use in an admissions appeal.

Other than the panel and clerk, is there anyone else at the hearing?

Yes. The only other person who must be at the hearing is a representative from the admission authority who will make the case for the authority. This person is referred to as the 'presenting officer'. The school may also be represented.

WILL I FIND OUT THE RESULT OF THE PANEL THAT SAME DAY?

No. They will typically contact you in writing but in some cases they may ask you to call the following day to find out the verdict.

I want my child to go to a particular school because it is clearly better than the rest. Is this a good enough reason?

No. Your local authority would state that any of the schools offered to your child would be of a good standard and meet the pastoral and academic needs of your child.

Can I appeal to more than one school?

Yes. If you have submitted appeals for more than one school, in general, they will be heard on the same day by the same panel, unless you state that you would prefer for them to be heard separately.

Will other parents appealing to the same school be present at my appeal?

No. Your appeal will be in private. However, several appeals will be heard in succession on the same occasion and the parents concerned may be together at the beginning of the session to hear general introductions and explanations.

How to further your chance of success in an appeal

▶ *Make sure you have a good case to start with – read through the school's admissions criteria carefully.*

▶ *Make sure you are aware of timings – you have a deadline to submit your appeal from receipt of your offer letter and there is also a deadline by which appeals should be heard after receipt of your appeal request.*

▶ *Ensure that your appeal submission has been received. You can do this either by hand delivering it and asking for a receipt or by asking the admissions authority to acknowledge receipt of it.*

▶ *Before the meeting, make sure you have all the supporting documents and written evidence to help your case.*

▶ *Don't forget about your child – make sure you discuss the issues and keep them strictly related to your child – how they would benefit from attending this school. Some parents forget to even mention their child in appeals!*

▶ *Bring a friend to give you support.*

▶ *Remember there are subtle differences in the administration of appeals in England, Scotland and Wales, so make sure you check up the latest procedures by reading your LEA's latest* Code of Practice.

▶ *Don't spend time discussing the unfairness of the system – this is outside the remit of the panel.*

▶ *Be realistic – most appeals are unsuccessful. The majority of cases which do get overturned are the ones with strong medical or social grounds.*

(Contd)

- *Don't be aggressive – it won't do you any good.*
- *Try to be neutral and don't disparage other local schools – it is possible that some of the panel may be associated with the other schools in some way.*
- *Role-play and practise what you are going to say to the panel with a friend first – this will give you more confidence at the appeal and keep you more focused and concise.*
- *Be honest – even if that means disclosing difficult and uncomfortable issues to the panel, such as domestic violence – they will understand and take these issues into consideration.*

10 THINGS TO REMEMBER

1 *Everyone has the right to appeal for a secondary school place.*

2 *You can appeal for more than one school.*

3 *There is always a deadline for appealing.*

4 *Appeal panels usually consist of three members, sometimes five.*

5 *Usually appeals are held between four and six weeks from the date you send your form to the clerk of the independent panel.*

6 *In order to win the appeal, you have to prove that the admissions arrangements were not correctly applied.*

7 *It is important to have evidence to back up your case.*

8 *It is helpful to go to an appeal with another person for emotional support.*

9 *There is seldom an advantage to bringing a lawyer or solicitor with you, as their legal knowledge may not be much use in an admissions appeal.*

10 *If you believe the appeals procedures were not correctly followed you can complain to the Local Government Ombudsman who will investigate the case.*

9

Advice for children with special educational needs and those with statements

In this chapter you will learn:

- *how to determine whether your child has special educational needs*
- *about the three stages of special educational needs identified in the* Code of Practice
- *how to decode some special educational needs jargon*
- *how the transition to secondary school is different for children with special educational needs.*

If teachers had a pound for every parent that told them their child had dyslexia they would all be very rich by now.

Unfortunately, not all parents understand what is meant by special educational needs (SEN) and feel that if their child is underperforming, they must have problems. This is not the case. Children develop at different rates and some children will take longer to develop and reach their potential than others. Alternatively, some children are just not high academic achievers and while appearing to make steady, slow progress they are still reaching their potential. Some parents find this very hard to accept and go looking for a problem that isn't there.

There is however, the other extreme where parents categorically deny the fact that their child may have special educational needs. This can be very difficult, as the individual measures which need to be put into place to support these children cannot be started without the approval of parents.

Defining special educational needs

So what are special educational needs and how will you know if this relates to your child? Special needs can be physical needs, emotional needs, social needs or behavioural needs. It is an umbrella term covering a wide variety of needs, ranging from mild learning difficulties to profound mental illness. Children with special educational needs have learning difficulties or disabilities that make it harder for them to learn than most children of the same age. It is the job of the school and the special educational needs co-ordinator (SENCO) to ensure that all children, including those with special needs, reach their full potential in school and are given access to a broad and balanced curriculum. Children with special educational needs experience a range of challenges, which may be in any of the following areas:

▶ *reading*
▶ *writing*
▶ *spelling*
▶ *numeracy*
▶ *social – making friends and interacting with others*
▶ *emotional and behavioural*
▶ *receptive and expressive language*
▶ *physical.*

Common examples of difficulties experienced by children with special educational needs within mainstream schools include attention deficit hyperactivity disorder (ADHD), autism, Asperger's Syndrome, dyslexia, dyspraxia and dyscalculia. Note that children are not considered to have special needs if they have learning difficulties due to English not being their first language. This is an English as an additional/second language (EASL) issue, not SEN.

What happens if my child is identified as having a special educational need?

By the time your child is at junior school you should have a pretty good idea whether they have special needs or not. Most schools have a special needs department, with a special educational needs co-ordinator (SENCO). It is their job to make provision for all children with special needs and this includes liaising with parents. Class teachers may have also raised concerns as your child progressed through school. The school must tell you when it starts giving extra or different help to your child because of their special educational needs. This may occur if a child shows signs of difficulty developing literacy or numeracy skills, or presents persistent emotional or behavioural difficulties, or has communication and/or interaction difficulties. This could take the shape of an extra 'intervention', where your child works in a smaller group or even in a one-to-one setting with a teacher or teaching assistant. It could be that the curriculum is differentiated to an extra level to meet the needs of your child or it could be that they are given extra equipment to help support them in class, such as a laptop computer or more concrete apparatus. At this stage – where your child's needs are being met within the school and classroom – your child will be put on the School Action stage. This is the first stage of special needs identified in *The Special Educational Needs Code of Practice* (2001), which is adopted in British schools. It is a way for schools and local authorities to monitor the progress of children with SEN, essentially tracking their progress via a register, or 'profile of concerns' which is regularly reviewed and updated.

If your child still does not make progress, specialist help may be requested from external services, for example: speech and language therapists, educational psychologists, physiotherapists, occupational therapists and so on. At this stage, your child will be put on the School Action Plus and an Individual Educational Plan will be written by their class teacher listing additional strategies, goals and targets to support your child in class. These are read and signed by parents and reviewed at least twice a year.

If your child continues to struggle at school the local educational authority may be requested by parents or the child's school to carry out a more detailed assessment of your child's needs. The authority might then write a statement of special educational needs, which describes the child's problems and all the special help they need. This is called a statement.

Insight

Statements are extremely hard to get, and getting even harder. Even over the last couple of years the number of children being given statements has dropped and support from the local authorities has dwindled. Sadly, this is all to do with funding and cutbacks.

Did you know?

▶ In January 2008, 223,600 (or 2.8%) of pupils across all schools in England had statements of SEN.
▶ An estimated one in five children has some form of special educational need, ranging from mild dyslexia to behavioural problems to complex medical conditions.
▶ The percentage of SEN pupils with statements in maintained secondary schools was 2% in 2007, down from 2.3% in 1997. The percentage of SEN pupils without statements was 16% in 2007, up from 15% in 1997.
▶ In 2008, the incidence of SEN pupils without statements was greater in primary schools (18.1%) than in secondary schools (17.8%).

Figures published by the Department for Children,
Schools and Families (June 2008)

Use the following list to clarify any unknown abbreviations!

SEN	special educational needs
SENCO	special educational needs co-ordinator
SPLD	specific learning difficulties
ASC	autistic spectrum condition
ADHD	attention deficit hyperactivity disorder
SA	School Action
SAP	School Action Plus
IEP	Individual Educational Plan
BESD	behavioural, emotional and social difficulties

How does the secondary school admissions process differ if my child has special educational needs?

How different the secondary school application procedure will be will depend on the needs of your child – and the stage they are at in the *Code of Practice*. As stated above, there are three stages of special educational needs which are followed in state schools. If your child is identified at the School Action or School Action Plus stage, then it is highly unlikely that their needs will change the whole entrance experience. Whether sitting for a state, state selective or private school your child will have to go through the same process as all other children. The only difference may occur if the needs of your child means they have to be dealt with in a different way, for example: they write slower than other children and thus need more time to complete the exam, or they need to be in a smaller room with fewer children due to anxiety or other medical conditions, such as ASC or ADHD. Some may need to use laptops in the exam. In cases such as these, parents are asked to put down in writing the special needs of their child and submit it to the

SENCO or head teacher of the secondary school who will decide on an individual basis how to meet the needs of these children.

Case study: grammar school prospectus (September 2008)

'If you think we need to make any special arrangements with regard to your child's application or to the entrance examination, please contact the Admissions Officer. Such requirements might include the following:

▶ *wheelchair access on the day of the examination*
▶ *enlarged type for examination papers*
▶ *a desk near the front of the examination room for the hearing impaired*
▶ *extra time because of specific learning difficulties.'*

CASE STUDY

Statemented children and secondary school admissions

The application process is totally different for statemented children, so it is really important for parents to be aware of their entitlement.

If your child is statemented, you have a right to say which secondary state school you want your child to go to, whether mainstream or special. Unlike the usual Common Application Form, there is a different form which needs to be filled in and only one school is requested. The local educational authority must go along with the parents' preference, as long as:

▶ *the school is suitable for the child's age, ability and needs*
▶ *admitting the child to the school won't harm the education of other pupils*
▶ *it is an efficient use of the authority's resources.*

Another notable difference is that children with statements find out which secondary school they have been given before the other children – essentially they are given priority and allocated first.

'Jack has mild ADHD and is possibly on the autistic spectrum.
We started looking at schools when Jack was in Year 5. As he had a
statement, we knew we had a passport to pretty much any state school
of our choice. I do believe it is very hard for a school to refuse a child
with a statement. It was lovely to be free of the worry of other parents
and all the cramming that was going on and exams being taken.
Of course we had our own worries, knowing full well that his learning
support assistant who had known him for years would be replaced by
many different assistants.

The school we chose is much sought-after in our borough and is very
strict with clear boundaries. It was really important that the three of
us were able, by appointment, to have our own personal guided tour
of the school with Jack asking as many questions as he wanted to.
I was also impressed by two things: the new SENCO came to his annual
review in March of Year 6 and the head of key stage 3 came to visit
all the Year 6 kids, in July, that were going to the school the following
September.

The school has a support suite designated to children with special
needs and a homework club. Jack uses the latter, which is open each
day until 4.30 p.m. and is a great help and reliever of stress and
arguments at home! I am happy with the communication between
myself and the school which is via phone or email.

It is hard to know what you will be up against until you are in the
system. It wasn't until Jack was in the midst of his end-of-Year 7 exams
that he complained of talking in the exam room. After investigating
I found out they put all the SEN kids together, regardless of their need.
So a highly-distracted boy with ADHD was placed in the same room –
albeit behind a partition – as children who needed assistants to read
out the question. I was dumbfounded. They tried to fob me off with
having no more spare rooms and it being a timetabling issue, but
after complaining I was reassured it would not happen again. Check
what subjects your child will be taken out of if they have to go for

extra support. Once again we are knocking our heads against a brick wall, as the only subjects they get taken out of are art, music and DT... we are talking about a boy who was born with a hammer in his hand. Remember a school is a business, giant industries that have to work like clockwork and cannot offer individual timetables, so check to see how flexible your choice would be.

Although we are pleased with the school, it is about weighing up the pros and cons. Unfortunately I do not think that a school exists that would be 100% perfect for children like Jack, who are the square pegs that we are trying to fit into the round holes of the state education on offer. I do wonder about independent schools too, not that we could afford it. Although they may offer smaller classes and possibly be more flexible with the curriculum, they may well lag behind with understanding special needs so I would advise anyone to research that really thoroughly.

On reflection, would we have chosen this highly selective oversubscribed school? I really don't know, but Jack is so happy there, enjoying his learning and is now making friends which counts enormously. Other schools would present other problems... I am sure the grass will always be greener. One thing is certain: it is important to be an assertive and proactive parent, battling your child's corner.'

Poppy, mother of Jack (Year 8)

Insight

I have found it helpful to compare state schools and private schools to the NHS and private hospitals. The private sector is very nice, but if you are really ill then you will want to be in the NHS sector with fully trained and experienced doctors and nurses to support you. This is the same with special needs education – state schools are far better equipped and have many more specialist professionals to support them than the private sector.

Frequently asked questions

Can I nominate an independent fee-paying school for my statemented child and will the local authority pay the bill?
Yes, and no! Parents with a statemented child have a right to request an independent school. Although the local authority will consider your request, it is not obliged to agree to such a request if your child's needs can be met in a mainstream maintained school or a maintained special school. Additionally, the local authority does not have the power to name an independent school on a child's statement against the school's wishes. However, there may be times when it is in the interest of the child to go to a particular independent school and in such cases the local authority will consider funding such placements.

Can I nominate a state selective school for my statemented child, even if my child does not meet the criteria for selection?
No. This is because the placement would not be suitable under the first SEN selection criterion, which is that it would be inappropriate to the pupil's ability.

Do private schools accept children with special needs?
Yes, but bear in mind that the child must pass their entrance examination. It is therefore more likely that the special needs of the child do not affect their academic ability, for example mild dyslexia or high-functioning Asperger's. These children may be offered more time in the examination.

Mainstream or special schools?

Many local authorities advocate that most pupils' special educational needs can be met equally well in a mainstream secondary school and are keen to urge parents to nominate their nearest mainstream secondary school. This is because they believe that this local school will be in the best position to retain friendship groups and minimize the stress that the change of school can bring. If you prefer, you may request a school that is outside your local authority and this school must equally accept your request, assuming the same three conditions mentioned previously are met. There are also mainstream schools with resourced specialist provision. This could be to support pupils with any number of special educational needs, for example: hearing impairment, emotional and behavioural difficulties, speech and language difficulties or autism. It is always worth checking with your local authority whether they have any specialist provision available in any of their mainstream schools.

Parent case study

'My son was diagnosed with Asperger's Syndrome in Year 3 and was given a statement by our local education authority in Year 4. Whilst I had given plenty of thought over which school would be the most suitable to meet his needs at secondary school, I didn't have a formal meeting with his primary school to discuss it openly until his annual review meeting in Year 5. At this meeting a member of the local authority attended, with the sole purpose to discuss secondary school options. I named a couple of schools that took my interest and she was able to advise me on the pros and cons of each school for meeting my son's needs. One of the schools was not in our local authority but I was told that this would not present a problem and that this school would prioritize a place for my son, unless there were a number of students applying at the same time all with the same needs as my son.

I also found talking to my son's head teacher helpful as well as the school SENCO. After the meeting I rang up these schools and spoke to the SENCOs there to see how they could address my son's needs. We decided to name the out-of-borough school as our preferred school and my son starts there in September.'

Jessie, mother of Jake (Year 6)

CASE STUDY

In some cases the school's admissions criteria favour pupils with special needs. You need to look this up when researching schools.

Secondary transfer and SEN children

▶ When choosing a school for your SEN child, talk to as many people as you can, including charities that specialize in your child's problem. Ask schools on your shortlist to advise you of their SEN policy.

▶ Know the system – find out which schools' admissions criteria favour pupils with SEN.

▶ Find out which mainstream schools have resourced specialist provision.

▶ Make contact with parents whose children have similar needs to your own and who have already transferred to secondary school. Find out first-hand about their experiences and how their school has met their child's needs.

10 THINGS TO REMEMBER

1 *The timings and deadlines for applying to secondary schools for children with a statement are different from those without a statement – they are usually submitted to the local authority earlier.*

2 *Parents of children with statements are allowed to nominate one preferred secondary school.*

3 *Parents of children with statements may nominate a private school, but it is unlikely that the local authority will provide for this as they may argue that the child's needs can be equally met at a state school.*

4 *The local educational authority must go along with the parents' preference as long as the school is suitable, admitting the child won't harm others and it is an efficient use of the authority's resources.*

5 *Children with statements find out about their secondary school place before other pupils. This is because these places are allocated first.*

6 *Unless your child has a statement, they will not be given priority for admissions based on their special needs and learning difficulties.*

7 *Parents of children with specific learning difficulties and/or a medical diagnosis such as dyslexia, ADHD or dyspraxia fill in the Common Application Form in exactly the same way as for other children without special educational needs.*

8 *Children with specific learning difficulties may be given extra time or support resources such as a laptop or a scribe to allow them to fully access the examinations.*

9 *When considering secondary schools for children with special needs, always ask to speak to the school's special needs co-ordinator and ask what provision they will make for your child.*

10 *State schools are often better equipped to provide special needs support to children than the private sector.*

10

How to prepare your child for secondary school

In this chapter you will learn:
- *how to help your child make new friends*
- *how to help your child know who and how to ask for help*
- *how to encourage your child to think positively*
- *how to assist your child with improving their preparation and organizational skills.*

So you think you've done the hard bit and it's easy from here on in... Think again! The last term in Year 6 at primary school is often an interesting mix of end-of-year productions, residential school trips and sex education. Throw in the end-of-year discos and developing hormones and it is a time bomb, ticking away, waiting to explode!

Don't despair – time is on your side. Use the last term at primary school and the summer holidays wisely so that your child can prepare for the demands and changes they will experience in secondary education. You will need to start giving them more independence; yes, they will need to start going out on their own and yes, this is every bit as terrifying as it sounds. Nonetheless, it is essential experience for secondary school.

By the beginning of March, subject to appeals, most of you will know which school your child will be attending come September.

All secondary schools promise a thorough handover. Some are more thorough than others. The handover may start early and it will take many different forms. A teacher from the new school may visit your child at their primary school or they might invite your child for an induction visit that could be a half day, a whole day – or even in some cases two days for more vulnerable special needs children. Either way, it's a great start but not enough. This chapter will tell you all you need to know as September fast approaches.

Identify your child's fears... and hopes

I worry about my overdraft. I worry about my job and I worry about my children all the time. It will come as no surprise that 11-year-olds worry about completely different things, but it never occurred to me to consider the fears my daughter was facing.

Pupil case study

'I was very nervous about going to secondary school. To start with, I was worried about the amount of pressure I would be under; by this I mean homework and always getting to lessons on time. I was also concerned about the older kids and what it would be like. My primary school was very small and in comparison my new secondary school seemed massive – who would be there for me if I needed help?'

Bailey (Year 8)

Sit down with your child in the Easter holidays of Year 6 and ask them what they are most looking forward to at their new school, and what are they most dreading. It'll be an eye opener. Of course, the obvious worries come out – homework, strictness of new teachers, getting lost and so on. But you might find some unexpected worries, such as one girl in my class who wrote that she was worried about her new school uniform; 'In what way?' I naively asked her, 'I might need to wear my skirt below the knee!' she replied, as if the answer was too obvious to be voiced.

Occasionally children will go into too much detail, with answers covering their fears over 'animal dissection' or 'blowing things up in chemistry'. For many, I suspect this would be more a hope than a fear!

Most frequent worries about secondary school

- getting lost
- getting a detention
- stricter rules and teachers
- too much homework
- having male teachers (for girls)
- uniform
- going to a single-sex school after a mixed primary school
- making new friends
- being late for school
- getting to school by public transport
- the new route to school
- learning the new school rules
- bullying
- the new, older children and being in the youngest year group again
- arriving late for lessons – being in the right place at the right time
- other children from other schools knowing more about certain subjects than they do
- not having the correct school equipment
- not keeping in touch with old school friends
- starting a new subject never taught before, for example a language.

Make sure you balance this discussion by asking your child what they are looking forward to most. Here are some examples:

- *making new friends*
- *wiping the slate clean/fresh start*

- *trying new things*
- *having new school lunches*
- *joining new clubs*
- *having a much larger variety of languages/subjects/lessons/sports*
- *having different teachers for each subject*
- *being more independent*
- *joining older siblings already at the same school.*

Whatever their worry, it should be taken seriously and discussed. A common worry for girls is having a male teacher at secondary school. It actually makes perfect sense – it is rare to have many male teachers at primary school – as men tend to prefer working at secondary schools or institutes for higher education. Those who do go into primary schools are often brilliant, but sadly few and far between. Therefore, girls may not experience input from male teachers until they are at secondary school and this can be a major cause of anxiety.

Another common worry is that of bullying. It is important to help your child to differentiate between bullying and falling out with someone – the anti-social behaviour needs to have three elements going on simultaneously for teachers to respond to it as bullying. Bullying needs to be deliberately hurtful behaviour, it needs to be repeated over a period of time and it needs to take place where it is difficult for those bullied to defend themselves. Many children confuse rows and arguments with bullying but it is not the same thing.

How to deal with your child's worries

There are many techniques you can use to deal with your child's worries. Talking about them is the obvious first step. You can encourage them to write their worry down on a sheet of toilet paper and flush it down the toilet. This can be very therapeutic, but you need to make sure that your child doesn't have too many worries as blocked toilets can be very expensive! Alternatively, you could attach a worry to a balloon and let it fly up into the sky. Or you could try a guided meditation in which they enter a beautiful peaceful garden and pin their worries to a worry tree, before exploring the garden.

In Guatemala, Central America, people believe that when you're upset or worried you tell a 'worry doll' your troubles. Legend has it that the dolls absorb your worries and allow you a worry-free day. You can buy them in some gift shops, or you can make a worry doll yourself by finding an old strip of fabric and winding a bit of cotton around the top of the fabric. At the top of the fabric, draw a face with a felt tip pen. You can give each doll one worry. Yes, this sounds totally weird, but it works and it is fun.

How to help your child make friends

We all need friends. Life would not be the same if we didn't have that special person in our day to share some of life's pivotal moments. For our children too, friends are important – inside and outside the classroom. Some people make new friends easily. Others will worry about it and find it much harder to find someone to talk to. Opposite is a list of handy tips to talk about with your child, to help them make new friends. Build up their confidence and remind them how good they are at making friends by using examples from their life.

Insight
I found it useful reminding my daughter that she had already made really good friends at primary school and that there was no reason why she wouldn't do the same at secondary school. I told her that everyone would feel a little anxious but that all the children were feeling the same way.

Suggestions for the first few days

- *Smile when someone says 'Hello'.*
- *Try to remember the other person's name.*
- *Try to be a good listener.*
- *Find out what you have in common.*
- *Make eye contact.*
- *Help others who might be a bit lonely.*
- *Hang out with people you think like you.*
- *Join a group – don't take it over.*
- *Ask questions about others' hobbies and previous schools.*

Role-play some initial ice-breaking conversations with your child before they start secondary school. Experience has shown that sometimes some of the questions children ask may seem innocent to them but are totally inappropriate and have a devastating effect on the further development of that particular friendship.

Spend some time with your child encouraging them to identify what is special about them and why they would make a good friend. This is an excellent activity to raise self-esteem. Encourage them to see how the way they behave impacts on the way other people behave towards them – they can change the way others respond to them by the approach they take towards others. For example, if a girl is shouting at your child, they could choose to shout back, which would lead to an argument. Alternatively, your child could choose to try to calm the other child down or walk away until the other child has had a chance to let their heated emotions subside. Remind them they have a choice.

Explain to your child that it is okay to not always agree with friends – variety is the spice of life and different points of view can be helpful. However, conflict can arise when one friend tries to convince the other that they are right. What must be taught is that we don't always have to agree with our friends but we do need to respect each other's differences. You may need to remind your child that one argument does not mean the end of the world.

There is often more than one solution to a problem. Rather than get into a stand-off, you might encourage your child to try a different approach to solving a problem. It can be very helpful seeking the advice of other friends – two heads are often better than one and can have a levelling effect when emotions run high.

Teach your child how to ask for help at a new school

For some people, asking for help is easy. Many enjoy playing the 'damsel in distress' card by simply flashing their eyelashes and feigning complete incompetence – well, not always feigning it! Nonetheless some people find it harder asking for help than others.

In a new school, children need help. This might make them feel nervous. They must learn who to ask for help as well as how to ask for help. To start with, brainstorm with your child different times they may need to ask for help.

I may need help in my new school:

▶ *when I get lost*
▶ *when I need to use the toilet during lesson time*
▶ *when I can't follow the new timetable*
▶ *when I forget my homework*
▶ *when I get hurt or feel ill*
▶ *when I don't understand something in class.*

Discuss with your child who they would go to in each situation – and if they don't know, it is important to find out before the need arises. Sometimes your child will need to interrupt an adult at school. To do this effectively your child first needs to assess the situation; is it a good time to disturb that adult and how important is the situation? If they deem it important, suggest to your child that they wait for a pause, make eye contact and politely use expressions like: 'Excuse me', 'Do you have a moment?', 'Pardon me' or 'May I ask a question?'

When your child needs to ask for help in class if they have not understood a question or task, they will need to ask clear questions. These could include: 'Can you repeat that again please?', 'Can you break the instructions down please?' or 'What does that mean?' It is important to acknowledge that simply asking a teacher to repeat a question in the same way is often not helpful – what the child needs the teacher to do is explain the question in a different manner.

Encourage your child to think positively

You don't need a degree in psychology to support your child through this important transfer. Nonetheless, using a bit of cognitive behaviour therapy always comes in handy when advising your child through the teething problems of starting a new school. A great deal of research has shown that the way we think about an event will affect the way we feel about the event. Therefore, all we need to do as caring parents is encourage our children to change the way they think and – hey presto – they will feel better about the event and the end outcome will be more positive.

This sounds easier than it is – especially when you have to start by encouraging your child to listen to voices in their head. No, it's true! We really do all talk to ourselves. Internal dialogue, or 'self-talk', is when we talk to ourselves about what has happened when problems arise. While these thoughts often go unnoticed, they have a profound effect on how we feel and act. Therefore the way we think affects how we feel.

All children are different and react differently to the same situation. However, if your child is anything like mine their self-talk will be things like: 'Why does this always happen to me?', 'I'm so unlucky' or 'It's always my fault'. Your job is to challenge these statements, to encourage your child to think differently about the situation; this will in turn help them to feel more positive.

Insight

I used to get a little frustrated when I picked up my daughter from school and listened to a long monologue of all the things that had gone wrong that day. I decided that it might help to ask her if anything had gone well. She seemed surprised at such a question and then nodded as if to say that went without saying. I believe it is really important to acknowledge the good parts of the day and not to dwell solely on the bad.

There are four approaches you can use to challenge the way your child is thinking:

▶ *Is it a global or specific situation – will it affect all areas of their life or is it particular to one setting, for example school or home?*
▶ *Is it an internal or external situation – involving only them or someone else as well?*
▶ *Is it a stable or unstable situation – is it unchanging and likely to stay the same or might it change or be variable?*
▶ *Is it a controllable or uncontrollable situation – can your child do anything about it or do they have no control over the outcome?*

For example, if a child says 'Everyone hates me' this statement is global, internal, stable and uncontrollable. Encourage your child to ask the following questions about this statement. Firstly, 'Does everyone really hate you?' This will change global into specific; your child will probably admit that not everyone hates them, just the other child they are having problems with.

Next ask: 'Is this friendship problem all about you, or does it involve others as well?' This will change the internal attribute to external. Others have a part to play in this problem as well. Will your child always be hated by everyone? Of course not. There is a particular problem that needs to be sorted, but events change and feelings change. It might be that choosing to play with others or challenging those they are having issues with will eventually lead to a change in the situation, thus it is unstable.

Finally, ask your child: 'Is there anything you can do about the situation? Do you have any control over it?' Almost always the answer will be 'Yes'. Encourage your child to play with others or assert themselves with those who are making them miserable. That way they exert some control over the situation that empowers them and makes them feel better. Thus from 'Everyone hates me', the thoughts can now be: 'I am having problems with Emily and Holly at school. This does not always happen; it is just happening now. The problem is not just my fault, but their fault too and I am able to take control of this situation by taking some sort of action.'

Take every situation and look at the problem, challenge the thinking and this can greatly help change the way your child is feeling.

Go from:

Problem	Thought	Feeling
My friends were upset I did not wait for them after school and don't want to be my friends any more.	'Everyone hates me.'	Sad and upset

To this:

My friends were upset I did not wait for them after school and don't want to be my friends any more.	'My friends are upset about a specific event. They think I don't care about them which is not true and so have been mean to me as they are feeling hurt.'	Okay

Go from:

Problem	Thought	Feeling
Jessie did not invite me to her birthday party.	'I'll never fit in.'	Sad and lonely

To this:

Jessie did not invite me to her birthday party.	'I never play much with Jessie and she probably was only able to invite very few friends to her party. Also, if I had to limit the number of people I could invite to my party I wouldn't invite Jessie but it does not mean I don't like her.'	Okay

How to improve your child's confidence

Confidence is a special quality. If it could be bought over the counter it would be one of the first things a parent would purchase for their child. The nature/nurture argument is still being debated regarding why some children grow up to be more confident than others but it is generally accepted that while some are born with more confidence than others, external, environmental factors do play a big part – and that means you! There are many things you can do to nurture your child's confidence:

1 *Encourage your child to know themselves. You might get a few surprises along the way. Don't assume your child is a carbon copy of yourself – take an interest in finding out who they really are. Ask them open questions about their likes and dislikes, ask their opinions on a variety of topics, including those to do with secondary school. It's okay to disagree with them; encourage them to debate their views, argue their points and challenge others' views. Tell them their strengths – compliment them but*

be specific. For example, don't just tell your child they look pretty; tell them why they look pretty: 'That yellow shirt brings out the golden highlights in your hair'. Don't just tell them they worked well on their homework; tell them you were impressed by the way they worked out the solution to the maths problem. Teach self-evaluation: encourage your child to assess their own behaviour and performance before you give your own judgements. Ask what they did well, and what could they have improved as well as what they liked and what they didn't.

2   Encourage your child to like themselves – this will build self-esteem and is an essential life skill. There are many things you can do to help increase your child's self-esteem. In isolation they may seem small but put together they are a powerful combination. Tips include:

    ▷ Frequently expressing your unconditional love, often giving clear and specific reasons. It's okay to explain that sometimes you might not like their behaviour – when they have just kicked a football through the living room window or forgotten to take their house keys to school – but you will always love them.

    ▷ Sharing the positive effect your child has on your life – let them know they make a difference.

    ▷ Demonstrating your trust by not interfering when it is not necessary.

    ▷ Being protective and angry on their behalf when they meet injustice. This shows that their thoughts and feelings matter.

3   Encourage your child to set real goals and targets. It is important for our children to feel they have some personal control over the world around them and this will increase their confidence. Goals need to be 'smart':

    ▷ Specific
    ▷ Measurable
    ▷ Achievable
    ▷ Realistic
    ▷ Time-bound.

They also need to be flexible, personal to them and respected by you.

4 *Encourage your child to be assertive. This quality allows children to achieve what they want in life without trampling on the needs and rights of others. Explain how a passive person responds to a situation and how an aggressive person responds. Children need to be able to identify that they have rights which should always be pursued but not at the cost of others.*

How to help your child become more organized

How often have you got to a place and realized you have forgotten something? Sometimes it's not a problem – you improvise – you borrow a friend's lipstick or you promise to bring the cheque with you next time. Sometimes, it's a bigger problem, such as going to the airport and forgetting your passport. Being organized is an essential part of day-to-day life and for the first time your child will begin to appreciate this. They can forget their homework in primary school and the world doesn't end. In secondary school the implications may be more serious. Every child has the same amount of time, but some manage to achieve far more in that time than others. Some are able to remember everything they need for the following day – others quite simply haven't got a clue.

Some parents leave nothing to chance. They interrogate their child before they step foot outside the front door – have they got their PE kit, homework, door keys, musical instrument, lunch money, trip money, nit letter, cornflakes packet for DT... the list is endless. If you are anally retentive you rummage through the empty cheese dipper pots in your child's school bag to claim any letters sent home from school; well, they brought it home in their bag – why expect them to physically hand it over to you?

It's okay to take the lead – it is extremely normal and common. However, doing the organizing for your child in secondary school will not help them – they now need to start taking control for themselves. Never do anything on a regular basis for your child that they are capable of doing for themselves. Your job is to assist them with this newfound independence – be their trainer, but don't do it for them.

How to get your child more organized

▶ Encourage your child to practise packing everything they need for the next school day in their bag. It is always best to do this the night before – we all know how things can get a bit manic in the mornings. Discuss the earlier start in the morning as this can be a big change for many primary school children. It is certainly worth investing in an alarm clock at this stage – some children may need their clocks set five minutes fast. Serious 'non-wakers' may even need more than one alarm clock set at five-minute intervals!

▶ Plan their route to and from their new school and practise it with them at first, then get them to do it on their own. This is one of the biggest anxieties children face and to have mastered it before the first day of term is a huge bonus.

▶ Encourage your child to go out more on their own before September so they are used to it before starting secondary school. Yes, I know... why give them independence when you would really prefer to wrap them up in cotton wool? The answer is because they will learn nothing about life wrapped up in cotton wool; now is as good a time as any to let them spread their wings. Obviously, when I suggest they start flying solo I don't mean completely solo – make sure they have a mobile phone with them for the numerous occasions when you ring them just to check they are breathing! On a more serious note, it is important to encourage your child to keep their mobile phone hidden when they're not using it and to think carefully before buying the latest phone model – this may attract potential thieves. You should also warn your child that using an iPod or MP3 player can be dangerous as it prevents awareness of what is happening around them. Remind your child to sit near

(Contd)

the driver or guard on public transport where possible and to avoid empty carriages on trains.

▶ Make sure your child knows both school and home phone numbers.

▶ Encourage your child to do their homework as soon as the work comes in; often it has to be done for the next day which can be very different from primary school. Also, don't let your child struggle on with homework for longer than the recommended time. If necessary, write a note on the homework confirming that the correct amount of time was spent on the task.

▶ Find an appropriate quiet working space in the house for your child to do homework.

▶ Locate internet access – secondary school homework can often require this. It can be at home or your local library or even at your child's school.

▶ Know the school rules regarding uniform (including jewellery, make-up, mobile phones, iPods and Game Boys).

▶ Practise putting on the school uniform – you'd be surprised at how difficult school ties can be.

▶ Make sure all equipment and uniform is named using either: marker pens, tape, labels or correction fluid.

▶ Warn your child that the school day will be very different from what they are used to. Some secondary schools have weekly timetables – some have fortnightly timetables. It is always helpful if you can get a copy of a timetable beforehand. It is unlikely it will be an up-to-date one as most schools like to plan their new timetables in the summer holidays but it will give your child a flavour of what their typical day may look like.

▶ Get a map of their new school and go through it with your child so they become familiar with the site – it is easy to get lost. If your child is a visual learner, it can be helpful to take photos of the different parts of the school in advance of arrival.

▶ Many schools will have Year 7 planners – these become the bible for new pupils when they start school and are a great way of preparing them. Try to get hold of one; if they have no spare copies, see if your primary school can get hold of one. All Year 7 planners tend to contain the same sort of information – so if you can get hold of any it is helpful.

▶ Always write down in your diary term dates and special events as soon as you receive the information – otherwise parents' evening can come and go without your ever knowing!

Parent case study

'I was really excited when my child, Briony, started Year 7, but I was nervous too. I thought it was important to try to keep positive, dealing with each new experience one by one.

Before she started in September we went through a few "what if" scenarios, for example: "What if you miss the bus?" or "What if you forget to bring in your lunch money?" This proved very useful as she was able to see that even in emergencies she would know what to do and was prepared.

Socially I tried to give her a head start too. Through the "parent grapevine" I found someone who lived locally who was starting the same school as Briony and I arranged a play date before term started – this local familiar face proved very helpful to Briony in her first few days.

Once she had started I encouraged Briony to be herself and whenever she experienced problems I tried to be upbeat, as I knew my anxieties would rub off on her. I explained to her before starting secondary school that initially it would feel strange and very different to her primary school. Trying to cope with new teachers, lessons, timetables and the travelling is a challenge and she would probably feel anxious. I emphasized to her that all the children would be feeling the same.

The first problem we encountered was when she was put in a different class to her former primary school friends – I told her not to get too upset as this would be an excellent opportunity to make friends with new people. I felt like a politician, spinning a negative into a positive!

(Contd)

At home I always allowed Briony chill-out time – she needed time to relax and unwind from her day before she could discuss it with me. Sometimes that meant waiting for her bedtime before the day's angst would seep out – sometimes it needed to even wait 'til my bedtime – but it needed to come out or it would build up inside of her.

Sometimes there are no solutions – but it helps to listen and let your child know you are there and their greatest supporter!'

Tania, mother of Briony (Year 7)

Sometimes it feels that when your child sneezes, you catch pneumonia – we feel it so much worse than they do. They bounce back but we take a lot longer to recover. Sometimes it is difficult to resist the urge to make voodoo dolls every time your child is upset by something at school – be it a spiteful friend or an unfair teacher. Resist you must... well most of the time anyway.

10 THINGS TO REMEMBER

1 *Start preparing your child for secondary school while they are still in Year 6.*

2 *Identify with your child their hopes and fears about going to secondary school and discuss them.*

3 *Explain to them that most children will be feeling as they are and that it is normal to have mixed feelings about starting a new school.*

4 *Making new friends is often an area of anxiety – remind your child about appropriate ways of making new friends and role-play scenarios with them if necessary.*

5 *Encourage your child to think positively and challenge any negative thoughts.*

6 *Discuss who they go to for help and where they go to for help in their new school.*

7 *Run through some 'what if' scenarios with your child.*

8 *Encourage your child to become more organized and start putting into place new routines while they are still in primary school.*

9 *Rehearse their new school journey well ahead of time.*

10 *Encourage your child to be more independent and suggest they start going out more regularly on their own.*

Taking it further

Useful resources

ACADEMIC ASSESSMENT

Surviving School Transfer is a consultancy for parents which offers testing, interviewing and a formal report giving full feedback on children's academic strengths and weaknesses. It also provides recommendations for the most suitable schools for transition. London based: www.katiekrais.com

APPEALS

The School Admission Appeals Code of Practice provides legal information about admissions and appeals from the Department for Children, Schools and Families: www.dcsf.gov.uk/sacode/

The Advisory Centre for Education (ACE) is a charity which provides advice and information on school admissions, and admission and exclusion appeals: www.ace-ed.org.uk

The Local Government Ombudsman provides independent investigations into complaints about appeals: www.lgo.org.uk

The Public Services Ombudsman for Wales provides independent investigations into complaints about school appeals: www.ombudsman-wales.org.uk

School Appeals provides help to assist you in winning school appeals: www.schoolappeals.org.uk

BURSARIES

ISBA (the Independent Schools' Bursars Association) is a charitable company limited by guarantee whose objects are the advancement of education by the promotion of efficient and effective financial management, administration and ancillary services in independent schools: www.theisba.org.uk/

The Educational Trusts' Forum offers information about the very wide variety of organizations which provide grants for a whole variety of reasons: www.educational-grants.org/

The Independent Schools Council provides information about scholarship and bursaries on offer: www.isc.co.uk/

COMMON ENTRANCE EXAMINATION PRACTICE PAPERS

The Independent Schools Examinations Board: www.iseb.co.uk

Bond free electronic materials: www.bond11plus.co.uk

Common entrance examination board past papers are available to order through Galore Park Publishing Ltd: www.galorepark.co.uk

11+ Practice Tests: www.elevenplus.com
W H Smith 11+ Practice Tests: www.whsmith.co.uk
Schofield & Sims: www.schofieldandsims.co.uk
Nelson Thornes Bond papers: www.nelsonthornes.com
GL Assessment papers: www.gl-assessment.co.uk
Letts Educational: www.lettsandlonsdale.com
Athey Educational: www.athey-educational.co.uk
CGP: www.cgpbooks.co.uk
Rising Stars UK Ltd: www.risingstars-uk.com
MW Educational: www.theeducationwebsite.co.uk
The Learning Together books: www.learningtogether.co.uk
R & S Educational Services: www.rseducation.co.uk

CURRICULUM INFORMATION

National Curriculum online provides details about the National Curriculum: www.education.gov.uk

The Qualifications and Curriculum Development Agency (QCDA) provides information about many aspects of the curriculum: www.qcda.org.uk

EDUCATION INSPECTORATES

Ofsted (The Office for Standards in Education in England): www.ofsted.gov.uk

Her Majesty's Inspectorate of Education in Scotland provides inspection reports for Scottish schools: www.hmie.gov.uk

Eystn (Her Majesty's Inspectorate for Education and Training in Wales): www.estyn.gov.uk

Independent Schools Inspectorate (ISI) who provide inspection reports for independent schools: www.isi.net

GENERAL PARENT HELP

Parentline Plus is a charity that provides help for parents: www.parentlineplus.org.uk

Choice Advisers are run by the local authority and give information about admissions procedures to parents. To find out more and locate your local Choice Advisers go to: http://choiceadvice.dcsf.gov.uk/dfes2

The Advisory Centre for Education provides a large amount of 11+ information ranging from details of school results and parent surveys to free downloads and an 11+ forum for parents: www.ace-ed.org.uk

Parentcentre provides general help and advice on parents' issues: www.parentcentre.gov.uk

Teachernet provides advice and guidance on a range of educational issues: www.teachernet.gov.uk

Parents in Touch provide guidance through all stages of education and child development: www.parentsintouch.co.uk

The National Confederation of Parent Teacher Associations is an organization which represents parents and teachers through PTAs: www.ncpta.org.uk/

The National Parent Partnership Network is a national organization supporting and enabling parents and carers of children with special educational needs and can be found by contacting your local authority or through www.parentpartnership.org.uk

Eleven Plus Advice provides parent advice on the 11+ exam, information and facts about the exams and recommended resources to help parents support their children: www.elevenplusadvice.co.uk

Mumsnet is a website with useful parenting tips and which brings mothers together to swap advice: www.mumsnet.com

Mind Being – hypnotherapist Sharon Waxkirsh offers useful therapy for both children and parents anxious about entrance exams: www.mindbeing.com

GOVERNMENT WEBSITES

Department for Education is the English government department for education: www.education.gov.uk

A comprehensive website giving information about all public services including many aspects of education: www.direct.gov.uk

Department for Children, Education, Lifelong Learning and Skills is the Welsh government's department for education: www.learning.wales.gov.uk

Sure Start is the Government programme which focuses on delivering the best start in life for every child. It brings together early education, childcare, health and family support: www.dcsf.gov.uk/everychildmatters/earlyyears/surestart

A school profile is an annual report for parents written by the schools themselves which contains information about the school. They can be read online at: http://schoolsfinder.direct.gov.uk/

Transport for London provides information about school transport for children in London: www.tfl.gov.uk

HOME EDUCATION

Education Otherwise provides advice for parents whose children are being educated outside of school: www.education-otherwise.org

The Home Education Advisory Service (HEAS) gives advice about home education: www.heas.org.uk

LOCAL AUTHORITIES

Your local authority will have a department which deals with local education issues, formally called the Local Education Authority or LEA.

PERFORMANCE TABLES

Government performance tables can be found online: www.dfes.gov.uk/performancetables/

The BBC website gives a good summary of the major league table issues and a breakdown of the crucial results: http://news.bbc.co.uk/1/hi/education/league_tables/default.stm

PRIVATE SCHOOLS ADVICE

The Independent Schools Council website: www.isc.co.uk

The website has a good parents' zone which offers advice, called ISCias: www.isc.co.uk/ParentZone_Welcome.htm

Information about the Common Entrance syllabus is available from the Independent Schools Examinations Board: www.iseb.co.uk

The Girls' Day School Trust (GDST) is the largest group of independent schools in the UK, with 4,000 staff and over 20,000 students between the ages of 3 and 18: www.gdst.net

The Scottish Council of Independent Schools (SCIS) provides information and profiles on independent schools in Scotland: www.scis.org.uk

Best-schools.co.uk provides internet information, advice and services to parents and pupils seeking a private education in the UK: www.best-schools.co.uk

UKPrivateSchools.com enables parents locally, nationally and globally to locate independent private schools which are most suitable for their children. The site has been developed by parents for parents: www.ukprivateschools.com

SCHOOL GUIDES

A comprehensive guide to all schools in the UK is: www.goodschoolsguide.co.uk

Schoolsnet provides detailed profiles on 27,000 schools: www.schoolsnet.com

Which School Limited is a directory of independent schools in the British Isles: www.isbi.com

Great Schools provides good schools advice for parents: www.greatschools.net

SPECIAL EDUCATIONAL NEEDS

The Tribunals Service is the government body that parents whose children have special educational needs deal with when appealing against decisions made by local authorities in England about their children's education: www.sendist.gov.uk

The Special Educational Needs Code of Practice outlines the government's commitment to providing equality of opportunity and high achievement for all children: www.teachernet.gov.uk

The Independent Parental Special Education Advice gives advice for children with special educational needs in England and Wales: www.ipsea.org.uk

Contact a Family is the only UK-wide charity providing advice, information and support to the parents of all disabled children: www.cafamily.org.uk

11+ practice material

The following pages contain sample material from 11+ exam papers, reproduced by kind permission of Bond, leading provider of practice papers.

These questions are taken from *11+ Test Papers: Mixed Pack 1 Standard Version*, first published in 2003 by Nelson Thornes Ltd

Edition used published in 2007 by Nelson Thornes Ltd, Delta Place, 27 Bath Road, Cheltenham, GL53 7TH, United Kingdom

ISBN 978 0 7487 8491 2

www.nelsonthornes.com/bond

English

Read the extract carefully, then answer the questions.

'The Silver Sword' by Ian Serraillier describes the plight of Ruth (12), Edek (11) and Bronia (3) who lived in Poland during the Second World War. These three children learnt what it really meant to survive after their father and mother were taken from them by the Nazis. The extract starts as they are fleeing from the house across the roof after the storm troopers had dragged their mother away and bundled her into a van, after locking the children in the house.

Luckily for them all the houses on this side of the road together were in one long terrace, otherwise they could not have got away. Even so, it was a miracle that none of their slips and tumbles ended in disaster.

They must have gone fully a hundred yards when the first explosion shook the air. A sheet of fire leapt up from their home into the frosty night sky. They fell flat in the snow and lay there. The roof shook, the whole city seemed to tremble. Another explosion. Smoke and flames poured from the windows. Sparks showered into the darkness.

'Come along,' said Edek. 'We shan't let them have us now.'

With growing confidence they hurried along the rooftops. At last, by descending a twisted fire escape, they reached street level. On and on they hurried, not knowing or caring where they went so long as they left those roaring flames behind them.

They did not stop till the fire was far away and the pale winter dawn was breaking.

They made their new home in a cellar at the other end of the city. They had tunnelled their way into it. From the street it looked like a rabbit's burrow in a mound of rubble, with part of a wall rising behind. On the far side there was a hole in the lower part of the wall, and this let in light and air as well as rain.

When they asked the Polish Council of Protection about their mother, they were told she had been taken off to Germany to work on the land. Nobody could say which part of Germany. Though they went many times to ask, they never found out any more. 'The war will end soon,' they were told. 'Be patient, and your mother will come back.'

But the war dragged on, and their patience was to be sorely tried.

They quickly made their new home as comfortable as they could. Edek, who could climb like a monkey, scaled three storeys of a bombed building to fetch a mattress and some curtains. The mattress he gave to Ruth and Bronia. The curtains made good sheets. On wet days they could be used over the hole in the wall to keep the rain out. With floorboards he made two beds, chairs, and a table. With bricks from the rubble he built a wall to divide the cellar into two rooms, one to live in and one to sleep in. He stole blankets from a Nazi supply dump, one for each of them.

Here they lived for the rest of that winter and the following spring.

Food was not easy to find. Ruth and Bronia had green Polish ration cards and were allowed to draw the small rations that the Nazis allowed. But, except when Edek found casual work, they had no money to buy food. Edek had no ration card. He had not dared to apply for one, as that would have meant disclosing his age. Everyone over twelve had to register, and he would almost certainly have been carried off to Germany as a slave worker. Whenever possible they ate at the soup kitchens which Polish Welfare had set up. Sometimes they begged at a nearby convent. Sometimes they stole from the Nazis or scrounged from their garbage bins. They saw nothing wrong in stealing from their enemies, but they were careful never to steal from their own people.

In early summer they left the city and went to live in the woods outside. It was cold at night out in the open. They slept huddled together in their blankets under an oak tree which Edek had chosen for the shelter of its branches. There was not much rain that summer, though they had one or two drenchings in May. After that Edek cut down some branches, lashed them together and made a lean-to. This was thick enough to keep out all but the heaviest rain.

From *The Silver Sword* by Ian Serraillier

1 Who was Bronia?
   A Edek's friend
   B A German guard
   C Edek's older sister
   D Edek's younger sister
   E Ruth and Edek's mother

2 In which country is this extract from the story set?
   A Poland
   B Switzerland
   C Germany
   D Great Britain
   E Austria

3 How did the children get away from the storm troopers?
   A by running into the cellar
   B by climbing across the roofs of buildings
   C by hiding in a garden
   D by disguising themselves as peasants
   E by mingling with the crowd of onlookers

4 Where did the children make their first home?
   A in a park
   B in a cellar
   C on the roof of a building
   D in a friend's house
   E in an old sports pavilion

5 Why did their new home look 'like a rabbit's burrow in a mound of rubble'?

   A It was in a building that had been damaged by bombs.

   B It was in a building that had been ruined during a storm.

   C It was in a building that had decayed over time and collapsed.

   D The children had tried to disguise it so they wouldn't be found.

   E The children tried to make it cosy like a burrow to help them stay warm.

6 What is the most likely reason for the Polish Council of Protection not giving the children more information about where their mother was?

   A They only gave information to adults.

   B The children couldn't afford the fee they charged for providing information.

   C With so many people missing they couldn't be sure where she was.

   D They had other more important things to do and didn't have the time to help the children.

   E The children were from a different city so they couldn't help them.

7 Why were the ration cards the children had been issued of little use to them?

   A They were out of date.

   B They could only be used if their mother was with them.

   C They only allowed the children to have food that they didn't know how to cook.

   D They could only be used in shops that were in another city.

   E They allowed them only very limited amounts of food.

8 Based on the information in the extract, what was the role of Polish Welfare?

   A To help people who wanted to move to Germany.

   B To raise money to help start rebuilding cities destroyed in the war.

C To help the Nazi government make sure Polish citizens followed their laws.

D To help Polish citizens who were in need as a result of the Nazis' actions.

E To keep track of Polish citizens who were missing.

9 Why do you think the children saw 'nothing wrong' in stealing from the Nazis?

A They knew the Nazis didn't like Polish food anyway.

B They didn't think that the Nazis would really mind.

C They thought that the Nazis would give them the food eventually anyway.

D They felt it was acceptable because the Nazis were the people who had caused them to go hungry and be without their parents.

E They believed that the food would just be wasted if they didn't take it.

10 What made Edek choose the tree he did for the children to sleep under?

A It was on a hill.

B It was close to water.

C It was away from other people.

D It provided protection from the weather.

E It was close to the paths they used to go into town.

11 What is the closest meaning to 'disclosing' (paragraph 11)?

A announcing

B revealing

C uttering

D registering

E writing

Answer the following questions about these words and phrases.

12 What class of words are these?

themselves   him   they   she

A adjectives

B common nouns

C verbs
D pronouns
E adverbs

13 Which of these lines from the extract includes a simile?
A In the early summer they left the city.
B Edek, who could climb like a monkey.
C Sometimes they begged at a nearby convent.

14 Which of these words from the extract is an abstract noun?

But the <u>war</u> dragged on, and <u>their</u> <u>patience</u> was to be <u>sorely</u> <u>tried</u>.
      A   B   C   D   E

In these sentences there are a number of spelling mistakes. Circle the letter where the spelling mistake is underlined.

15
<u>Although they were determined</u> <u>to withstand the terrible deprivations</u>
A   B
<u>they longed for a</u> <u>more comfortable enviroment</u>.
C   D

16
<u>Little did she realize</u> <u>the invaders' behavour</u> <u>was going to be the</u>
A   B   C
<u>catalyst</u> <u>for so many tragic events</u>.
          D

17
<u>There was to be a cataloge</u> <u>of disasters on a scale</u> <u>that in normal times</u>
A   B   C
<u>would have been considered incomprehensible</u>.
D

Circle the letter below the word or words that need to be chosen for the extract to make sense and use correct English.

18 Whose kite flies <u>high</u> <u>higher</u> <u>highest</u> <u>more higher</u> <u>most higher</u>,
                      A   **B**   **C**   **D**   **E**
yours or mine?

19 The children <u>did</u> <u>had did</u> <u>done have did</u> <u>did done</u> their best to
                 A **B**   **C**   **D**   **E**
keep warm.

20 My friend <u>which</u> <u>that</u> <u>whose</u> <u>who</u> <u>what</u> lives next door plays
              A   **B**   **C**   **D** **E**
very loud music.

Maths

Answer the following questions without using a calculator.

1

Which quadrilateral does not have an obtuse angle?

Answer _____

2 Mrs Woodside is organizing a school trip. Each child needs to pay £x for the transport. Each child also has to pay £y for the accommodation. If there are 45 children going on the trip how much will the total payment be?
  A $45 + x + y$ **B** $45x + y$ **C** $x + 45y$ **D** $45(x + y)$
  E $45xy$

3 This graph is used to convert kilograms to pounds. Using the graph, write approximately how many pounds is 200 kilograms.

A 44 pounds
B 94 pounds
C 404 pounds
D 400 pounds
E 440 pounds

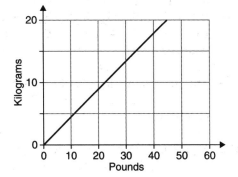

Kilograms / Pounds

4

A   B   C   D   E

Only one of the above diagrams is the net of a closed cuboid. Which net can be folded to form the closed cuboid?

5 Jamie has a collection of antique comics. He has three worth £4.75 each, seven worth £3.20 each, and 12 worth £2 each. How much is his total collection worth?

Answer _____

6 5^4 = ?
A $4 \times 4 \times 4 \times 4 \times 4$ B $5 \times 5 \times 5 \times 5$ C 5×4 D 54   E 45

7 3.344670 What is this number to two decimal places?

Answer _____

8 A map of Belgium is drawn to a scale of 1:175,000. How many centimetres on the map would show 35 km?

    35 cm   20 cm   17.5 cm   2 cm   3.5 cm

9 Which fraction has the smallest value?

    A $^4/_7$ **B** $^7/_{12}$ **C** $^4/_6$ **D** $^9/_{16}$ **E** $^5/_8$

10

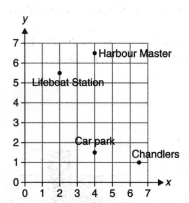

Write the co-ordinates of the Harbour Master.

Answer (,)

11 These are the numbers of letters received by the school office each day for a week.

    13   8   21   5   20

What is the median number of letters?

A 21   **B** 13   **C** 67   **D** 12   **E** 20

12 Which of these shapes has rotational symmetry?

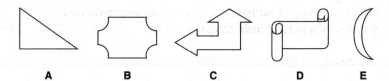

    A   B   C   D   E

Answer _____

13 Tina buys a new rucksack for school. She buys the largest one she can find. What is the size of her rucksack likely to be? Underline the most sensible answer.

1 litre

0.35 litres   3.5 litres   35 litres   350 litres   3,500 litres

14 Rosa thinks of a number. She doubles it, then multiplies it by 4. She then divides this number by 8. The result is 3. What number did Rosa first think of?

Answer _____

15 This bar chart shows the number of lengths swum in a sponsored swim. How many people swam 30 or more lengths?

Answer _____

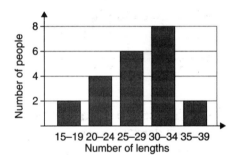

16 Here are the months of the year:

January   February   March   April   May   June
July   August   September October   November   December

As a percentage, how many months of the year have an even number of letters in their names?

Answer _____

17 y is equal to $\frac{3}{4}$ of x. Which of the following is incorrect?

A $4y = 3x$ **B** $\frac{y}{x} = \frac{3}{4}$ **C** $3y = 4x$ **D** $y = \frac{3}{4}x$ **E** $x = \frac{4}{3}y$

18 192 flights leave Newtown Airport each day. 5/8 of them are international flights, the others are domestic flights. How many domestic flights leave Newtown Airport each day?

Answer _____

19 A bag contains some coloured pencils. There are:
two black   three red   four blue   five green   six yellow
What is the probability that I don't pick a red?

Answer _____

20 The area of a rectangle is 36 cm². What could be the perimeter of the rectangle?

A 6 cm **B** 9 cm **C** 12 cm **D** 18 cm **E** 26 cm

_____

Verbal reasoning

Underline the two words which are the odd ones out in the following groups of words.

1 wolf   tiger   lion   panther   bear
2 chair   table   sofa   window   stool
3 rock   mud   dirt   soil   stone

Give the answer to each of these calculations as a letter.

If a = 20, b = 10, c = 5, d = 4 and e = 2:

4 (a + c) ÷ c = _____
5 3b − 5e = _____
6 b² ÷ a = _____

Underline the two words, one from each group, which are the most opposite in meaning.

7 (hamper, assist, support)   (pretend, help, escape)
8 (annoy, troubled, itchy)   (content, furious, irritate)
9 (extreme, fulfil, endless)   (complete, first, limited)

Read the first two statements and then underline one of the four options below that must be true.

10 Monet painted poppies. He was born in France.

    Pictures consist of paint.
    Monet liked poppies.
    Monet was a French painter.
    Poppies grow in France.

Write the two missing pairs of letters in the following sequences. The alphabet has been written out to help you.

A B C D E F G H I J K L M N O P Q R S T U V W X Y Z

11	BG	BI	CK	CM	___	___
12	___	VU	TS	RQ	PO	___
13	BD	EG	___	KM	___	QS

Find the four-letter word hidden at the end of one word and the beginning of the next word. The order of the letters may not be changed.

14 Listen to her advice carefully._____
15 Come to the back door of the new building._____
16 Take your litter home, never drop it._____

17 Class 1 was doing a survey of favourite drinks. Here are the results of one group:

    Paul and Judy like tea, squash and cola.
    Peter, Tanya and Toby like lemonade.

Suzy and Jon like squash, lemonade and juice.
Emily, Sue and Kamal like cola and milk.
All the girls also like soda water.

Which people like lemonade but not soda water? _____

Underline two words, one from each group, that go together to form a new word. The word in the first group always comes first.

18 (sun, cloud, rain)   (shone, fall, pour)
19 (act, play, sausage)   (role, cast, room)
20 (for, four, fore)   (gear, place, leg)

Move one letter from the first word and add it to the second word to make two new words.

21 duet   sing   _____   _____
22 fright   time   _____   _____
23 please   sill   _____   _____

Complete the following sentences in the best way by choosing one word from each set of brackets.

24 Minute is to (hour, tiny, second) as vast is to (clock, time, huge).
25 Bird is to (nest, talon, worm) as frog is to (wet, hop, fly).
26 Window is to (view, curtain, glass) as door is to (visitor, wood, hall).

Underline the two words, one from each group, which are closest in meaning.

27 (surge, blanket, touch)   (pillow, swell, creep)
28 (find, decipher, lift)   (lose, crack, destroy)
29 (cloud, mop, pail)   (bucket, whiten, light)

Find the three-letter word which can be added to the letters in capitals to make a new word. The new word will complete the sentence sensibly.

30 May I borrow your NIS racket please? _____
31 Michael was SDING at the corner of the street. _____
32 Please peel an OGE for your sister. _____

Find the letter which will complete both pairs of words, ending the first word and starting the second. The same letter must be used for both pairs of words.

33 pur___eed   bea___ope
34 see___ept   ban___eep
35 ple___ble   are___rch

Write the two missing numbers in the following sequences.

36	14	17	16	12	___	___
37	64	___	16	8	4	___
38	10	___	12	13	___	11

Change the first word of the third pair in the same way as the other pairs to give a new word.

39 belt, bash   welt, wash   melt, _____
40 rail, rain   pail, pain   mail, _____
41 latest, late   ballot, ball   offer, _____

Look at the first group of three words. The word in the middle has been made from the other two words. Complete the second group of three words in the same way, making a new word in the middle.

42 PAIN   PART   SORT   CART   _____   BIKE
43 NEED   BIND   BINS   MOVE   _____   TIES
44 COAT   CUTE   HUGE   BOOT   _____   FEES

Non-verbal reasoning

SECTION 1

Which shape or pattern completes the second pair in the same way as the first pair?

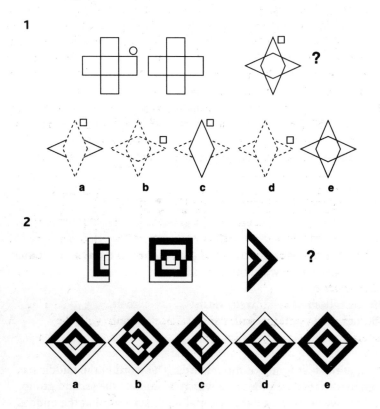

3

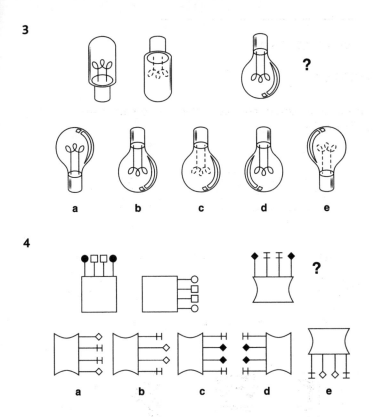

4

SECTION 2

Which shape or pattern from the second set belongs with the first two?

1

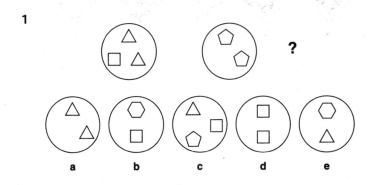

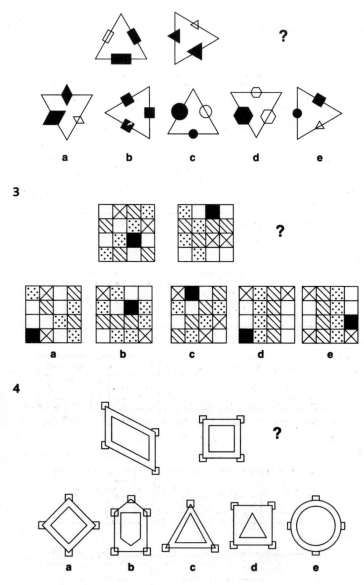

2

3

4

SECTION 3

Which one comes next?

1

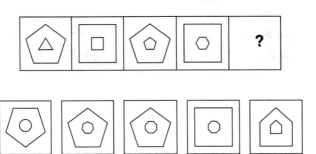

2

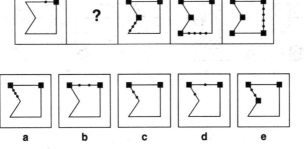

3

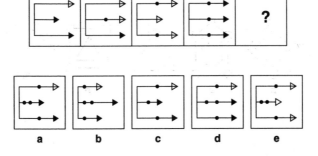

4

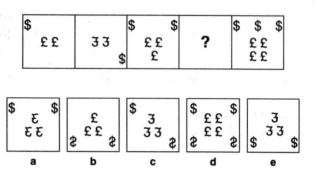

SECTION 4

Which code matches the last shape or pattern?

1

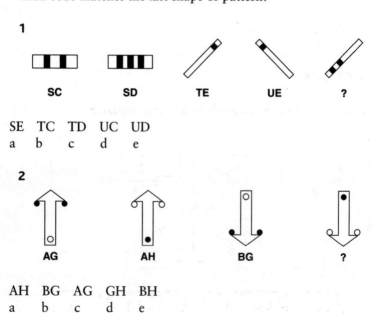

| SC | SD | TE | UE | ? |

SE	TC	TD	UC	UD
a	b	c	d	e

2

| AG | AH | BG | ? |

AH	BG	AG	GH	BH
a	b	c	d	e

3

XL   YM   ZL   ?

XM   YM   YL   ZM   XL
a   b   c   d   e

4

HV   IW   JW   ?

HW   IV   IW   JV   HV
a   b   c   d   e

SECTION 5

Which shape or pattern completes the larger square?

1

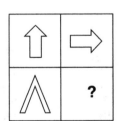

a   b   c   d   e

2

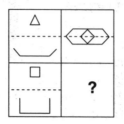

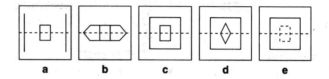

3

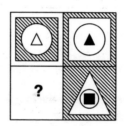

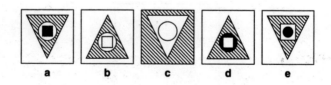

222

4

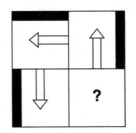

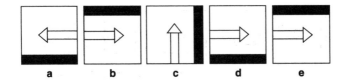

a   b   c   d   e

Answers

ENGLISH

1 D	**2** A	**3** B	**4** B
5 A	**6** C	**7** E	**8** D
9 D	**10** D	**11** B	**12** D
13 B	**14** C	**15** D	**16** B
17 A	**18** B	**19** A	**20** D

MATHS

1 E	**2** D	**3** E	**4** D
5 £60.65	**6** B	**7** 3.34	**8** 20 cm
9 D	**10** (4, 6.5)	**11** B	**12** B
13 35 litres	**14** 3	**15** 10	**16** 50%
17 C	**18** 72	**19** 17/20	**20** E

VERBAL REASONING

1 wolf, bear
2 table, window
3 rock, stone
4 c
5 a
6 c
7 hamper, help
8 troubled, content
9 endless, limited
10 Monet was a French painter.
11 DO, DQ
12 XW, NM
13 HJ, NP
14 tent
15 then
16 omen
17 Peter, Toby, Jon
18 rainfall
19 playroom
20 foreleg
21 due, sting
22 fight, timer

23 lease, spill
24 tiny, huge
25 worm, fly
26 glass, wood
27 surge, swell
28 decipher, crack
29 pail, bucket
30 TEN
31 TAN
32 RAN
33 r
34 k
35 a
36 18, 7
37 32, 2
38 15, 14
39 mash
40 main
41 off
42 CAKE
43 TIME
44 BETS

NON-VERBAL REASONING

Section 1
1 e   2 a   3 e   4 a

Section 2
1 b   2 a   3 d   4 a

Section 3
1 b   2 c   3 a   4 e

Section 4
1 b   2 e   3 a   4 b

Section 5
1 b   2 c   3 b   4 d

Index

Image credits

Notes

Notes

Notes

Notes

Notes

Notes